JACOB VINER

JACOB VINER
LECTURES IN
ECONOMICS 301

Douglas A. Irwin and
Steven G. Medema, editors

Transaction Publishers
New Brunswick (U.S.A.) and London (U.K.)

Library of Congress Catalog Number: 2012036967
ISBN: 978-1-4128-5166-4
Printed in the United States of America

Library of Congress Cataloging-in-Publication Data

Viner, Jacob, 1892-1970.
  Jacob Viner : lectures in economics 301 / Douglas A. Irwin and Steven G. Medema, editors.
      p. cm.
  Includes bibliographical references and index.
  ISBN 978-1-4128-5166-4
  1. Economics. 2. Economics—Study and teaching (Higher) I. Title.
  HB171.V48 2013
  330—dc23

                                              2012036967

Contents

Acknowledgments

Materials from the Jacob Viner Papers are used with the permission of Princeton University. The editors are grateful to the staff of the Seeley G. Mudd Manuscript Library at Princeton for their assistance with these materials and for permission to quote from them in the editor's Introduction. The editors would also like to thank Rodney Spencer for his excellent work in translating Ketchum's hand-drawn graphs into the finished products that can be observed here.

The late Irving Louis Horowitz, Transaction's longtime chairman, was keen on publishing these lectures, which form an important part of the Transaction's series of classic works in the Chicago price theory tradition—a series that also includes Frank H. Knight's *The Economic Organization*, Milton Friedman's *Price Theory*, and Gary S. Becker's *Economic Theory*. The editors are grateful for Horowitz' encouragement of this project; for the efforts of Andrew McIntosh, their editor; and to the rest of the staff at Transaction for seeing this project through to completion. We also thank Maha Malik, a student at Dartmouth, for her assistance in preparing the index.

Introduction[*]

Douglas A. Irwin and Steven G. Medema

The important place that the University of Chicago occupies in the history of twentieth-century economics is validated by its numerous Nobel Prizes and reflected in the numerous studies of the "Chicago School" undertaken by historians of economics. One of the most significant aspects of this history lies in the Chicago price theory tradition—a tradition that has its genesis with Frank H. Knight and Jacob Viner in the 1920s, continues most prominently today in the work of Steven Levitt of *Freakonomics* (2005) fame, and which has been institutionalized through the founding, in 2004, of the Becker Center on Chicago Price Theory at the University of Chicago.[1] While the post–World War II Chicago of Milton Friedman, George Stigler, Ronald Coase, Gary Becker, and Robert Lucas receives the most attention from historians of economics these days, the prewar department continues to attract attention from scholars. In the 1930s, Chicago was, as Paul Samuelson (1972, 5) pointed out, "the best Department of Economics in the country," a reputation that was due to both its masterful faculty and the exceptionally able students it produced.[2]

Even in this earlier era, the department was especially known for instilling in its students a thorough understanding of price theory—largely at the hands of Knight and Viner. The hallmark of this inculcation was Econ 301, the core graduate course in price theory that long differentiated the Chicago approach to what is more commonly known as "microeconomics" from the courses being offered in other leading economics departments. Such was the centrality of this course for the training of a Chicago economist that only five individuals were regularly assigned to teach this course between the late 1920s and 1980: Frank Knight, Jacob Viner, Milton Friedman, Arnold Harberger, and Gary Becker (Emmett 2011).

The Chicago price theoretic approach was brought to the Law School in the 1930s in the person of Henry Simons—Knight's prized student—and then by Aaron Director after Simons' death in 1946. Though the Chicago price theory tradition exhibits elements of continuity and change over the course of its roughly ninety years, one constant view has been that, at Chicago, a form of price theory was being practiced that was self-consciously different from that being practiced in the profession at large. The main thrust of the Chicago price theory tradition was an emphasis on Marshallian, partial-equilibrium economic reasoning, and the use of this reasoning to understand real-world phenomena. This was true as against the institutionalist approach that loomed large in the 1920s and 1930s, the monopolistic competition revolution of the 1930s and 1940s, the mid-century ascendancy of Walrasian general equilibrium analysis, and the more recent game-theoretic and set-theoretic turns which have become fashionable in the field.[3]

The literature to date on Chicago price theory in the pre–World War I period has tended to focus on the work of Frank Knight and his student, Henry Simons, to the relative neglect of Jacob Viner.[4] However, Viner made important contributions to price theory scholarship and was known as a brilliant teacher of the subject—one whose approach had a powerful impact on his students. We have a good sense for the content of the price theory courses offered by Knight, Friedman, and Becker from their price theory "texts" and (in the case of Knight and Friedman, at least) from copies of student notes that have survived.[5] Likewise, George Stigler's approach to the subject is masterfully laid out in *The Theory of Competitive Price* (1942) and the four subsequent editions published under the more abbreviated title, *The Theory of Price*.[6] Although it has been clear for many decades that Viner's influence looms large in the Chicago price theory tradition, what has been missing from the public view, until now, is a good sense for the exact nature of his contribution.

In his 1972 remembrance of Viner, Paul Samuelson, who attended Viner's Econ 301 course as an undergraduate in 1935, mentions a particular set of notes taken from Viner's lectures on price theory "around 1930," a mimeographed copy of which was placed on deposit for student use at the University of Chicago's Harper Library (1972, 7). These notes, it turns out, were not merely random student scribblings; rather, they were a nearly verbatim transcription of the lectures that Viner had delivered in Econ 301 during the summer term of 1930. This volume brings these notes to publication as a part of a larger process of publishing or reissuing various classics in Chicago price theory—a project that includes Friedman's *Price Theory* (Transaction edition 2007) and Becker's *Economic Theory* (Transaction edition 2007) and which, we hope, will soon include Knight's *The Economic Organization* and one of the editions of Stigler's classic treatise.

In the remaining sections of this introduction, we will present a brief précis of Viner's career and from there, move on to a discussion of Viner's manner of teaching. Finally, we will elaborate on the story of the notes, which one of us (Irwin) rediscovered twenty seven years ago, and provide an overview of their contents.

A Précis of Viner's Career

Born in Montreal, Canada, in 1892, Viner took his B.A. from McGill University in 1914 and moved from there to Harvard, where he studied under the illustrious American Marshallian, Frank Taussig. Viner left Harvard for Chicago in 1916 and did not complete his Ph.D. dissertation until 1922. Though his stay at Harvard was relatively brief, Taussig's influence pervaded Viner's scholarship and teaching, and this influence can be seen very clearly both in Viner's seminal work in international economics and in his approach to price theory.

Viner's initial appointment at Chicago was as an instructor for the academic year 1916–1917, after which he served for a time at the US Tariff Commission and the Shipping Board. He returned to Chicago in 1919 and remained on the faculty there, with brief interruptions for government service or to take up visiting positions at other universities, until his departure for Princeton in 1946. His strong attachment to the University is evident from the many important university committees on which he served and the effort that he devoted to this work.[7] The stimulating intellectual environment provided by the Chicago department was something that he valued highly, and his eighteen-year editorship of the *Journal of Political Economy* (1928–1946) raised the journal's prestige in the eyes of the profession to a great extent.

During his time on the faculty, Viner was one of the most illustrious members of the Chicago economics department.[8] This is no small thing, given that his colleagues at Chicago included luminaries such as Knight, Simons, Lloyd Mints, Harry Millis, Paul Douglas, Simeon Leland, John Maurice Clark, Henry Schultz, Jacob Marschak, and T. W. Schultz. However, as Simon Leland later noted, "The brightest star in this galaxy was Viner."[9] Viner left his imprint across the department, the profession, and beyond, and he did so in a variety of ways—through his teaching of the next generation of Chicago economists, his wide-ranging contributions to scholarship, his editorship of the *Journal of Political Economy*, and his service on governmental boards and commissions.

Although Viner is most famous for his work in international economics and intellectual history, his contributions range across the field of economics, including price theory, as his classic article "Cost Curves and Supply Curves" in 1931 attests[10]; macroeconomics, where he was an early advocate of deficit-financed stimulus measures; monetary policy; and economic methodology.[11] The influence of this work is reflected in Viner's receipt of numerous academic and professional honors: He was elected president of the American Economic Association for 1939, named a fellow of the American Academy of Arts and Sciences and the British Academy, was an elected member of the American Philosophical Society and the Royal Academy of Sweden, and received numerous honorary degrees. The most important of these many honors came in 1962, when Viner was named the fourth recipient of the Frances A. Walker Medal—a prize given every five years by the American Economic Association "to the living American economist who in the judgment of the awarding body has during his career made the greatest contribution to economics."[12]

Viner as Teacher

Along with Frank Knight, Viner was responsible for the introductory graduate price theory course from the 1920s until his departure for Princeton in 1946—at which point Friedman assumed the teaching of the course. Viner's course was taken by students whose ranks included Samuelson, Friedman, Stigler, Kenneth Boulding, Allen Wallis, Martin Bronfenbrenner, Don Patinkin, and many others. Viner shared with his mentor, Frank Taussig, the love of teaching and the gifts for it, and most students who took Viner's course were impressed by his erudition and stimulated by his classroom instruction. As the editors of the *American Economic Review* mentioned in their memorial tribute to Viner, his course gave the students

> a feeling for the subtlety, power, and appeal of pure economic theory. In Viner's hands, economic theory was not a set of formal abstract propositions; it was a set of tools, to be constructed with care and the utmost attention to logical rigor, but to be judged primarily by its usefulness in understanding and interpreting important economic phenomena. He presented economic theory as, in Marshall's words, 'an engine of analysis.' And he presented it with verve and color, making it an exciting and controversial subject. He had few peers for quickness of mind and tongue or ability to grasp new ideas or to spot and expose fallacies (*AER* 1971, 247).

Much the same was later said about Friedman's Economics 301 course, which bears Viner's imprint. Indeed, Friedman later remarked that Viner's class, which he took in the fall of 1932, "opened up a new world. He made me realize that economic theory was a coherent, logical whole that held together, that it didn't simply consist of a set of disjointed propositions. That course was unquestionably the greatest intellectual experience of my life" (Breit and Hirsch 2009, 70).[13] Though Samuelson was to take economic theory in a rather different direction from that espoused by Viner, he remarked on multiple occasions about the profound effect that Viner's course had on him. "By reputation," he said in 1972, "it was considered the best course in economic theory being given in the America of those days. On reflection, I think it probably deserved that accolade" (1972, 6).

The notoriety and legendary status of Viner's course was due in no small part to its place as the challenging bottleneck course that was necessary for further progress in the doctoral program in economics—the "Holy of Holies at the Univ. of Chicago," as Samuelson put it in 1962.[14] Samuelson recalls the presence that Viner had in the classroom:

> He was short and intense, like a bantam cock. His upper lip, usually bedewed by a bead of moisture, curled in what seemed a half smile. In my imperfect memory, his hair was then red, and his complexion matched. His suit coats were on the short side and his posture was not that of a West Point cadet. (1972, 6)

Viner practiced the Socratic method of his mentor, Taussig, but to it, according to Samuelson, Viner added "terror." Samuelson described the daily setting as follows:

> Members of the seminar sat tensely around a table, and when the name of the victim was read off the cards, you could almost hear the sighs of relief and the slumping back into chairs of those who had won temporary respite. Indeed, the stakes were high. Three strikes and you were out [of the course], with no appeal possible to any higher court. And this was no joke. (1972, 6)

Indeed, Samuelson reports that many of his classmates were ejected from the course on these grounds.[15]

Martin Bronfenbrenner (1982, 348) has memories of the course that parallel those of Samuelson, noting that

> budding Chicago economists of those years trembled in the presence of the ferocious Jacob Viner. Viner could (and did) end careers by ejecting some aspirant "not ready" for his required theory course, "Econ. 301," as when said aspirant could not "go to

the board and draw that" (meaning some confused nonsense said aspirant had just fumbled forth).

George Stigler (1988, 19–20), no shrinking violet himself, recalled that Viner was "a stern disciplinarian in the classroom" and relates the following story:

> In an early session of his famous course on economic theory, Economics 301, in 1934, Viner asked one student what factors determined the elasticity of demand for a product. After a sensible beginning about the availability of substitute products, the student added "the conditions of supply." Viner turned red and said, "Mr. X, you do not belong in this class." My spine, and probably all of those in the class, began to tingle.

In truth, Viner had been entrusted by the department with the task of using this course to weed out students who were not sufficiently able, and this was, says Samuelson, "not work for which he was unfit" (1972, 6).

Simeon Leland (n.d., 2) suggests that Viner mellowed in the classroom as the years went by[16]; other students of Viner with whom Irwin has spoken do not remember Viner as being excessively sharp-tongued or fear inducing. Though known as a rigorous and exacting grader, Viner was also regarded as being eminently fair in these evaluations and was known for spending many hours in pouring over his students' papers and examinations. The fact that roughly thirty students wrote their Ph.D. dissertations under his supervision during this time at Chicago attests to the fact that although his standards inside and outside of the classroom were very high, the students understood and valued what Viner had to offer.

The Origin of the Notes

It is by now well known that Friedman's *Price Theory* (1962) textbook evolved from a set of student notes taken by David Fand and Warren Gustus and circulated in mimeographed form among graduate students at Chicago for a number of years before Friedman agreed to edit them for publication. Samuelson's 1972 memorial tribute to Viner provided a hint of a similar set of notes from Viner's course:

> To my regret, the notes that I took for Viner's course, if they still exist, are not in any location known to me. But that is perhaps just as well, for Viner was vehement in his belief that it was a sacrilege to take skimpy notes from a course and present it to the world as a fair sample of the course's quality. To his indignation, a student had done just that around 1930, and a mimeographed copy of the notes was on deposit in Harper Library (1972, 7).

It is understandable that a scholar of Viner's meticulousness would be leery of such notes. "To buttress his sensitivity on this point," Samuelson continues, "Viner made reference to Wesley Mitchell's famous course at Columbia" on the history of economic thought where "Without authorization a student circulated rather elaborate mimeographed notes," which were later published. Samuelson reports that Viner found these notes "extremely disappointing" and laid the blame on the note taker rather than on Mitchell himself (1972, 7).[17]

About twenty seven years ago, Irwin found a copy of the notes mentioned by Samuelson in the Columbia University Business Library. They cover the Economics 301 course that Viner taught during the summer quarter in 1930. The notes were in good condition (having been examined infrequently, we suspect), although some of the yellowed pages were beginning to crumble. The mimeographed sheets, with lecture dates beginning on June 17 and ending on August 27, consist of 117 single-spaced typed pages, including diagrams. The title page reads: "Lectures in Economics 301—Price and Distribution Theory by Jacob Viner, M. D. Ketchum (Editor)." A bit of digging in the Jacob Viner Papers at Princeton University's Seeley G. Mudd Manuscript Library allowed Medema to unearth a brief correspondence between Ketchum and Viner from 1930 and 1931 that pertains to these notes, a correspondence which suggests a lack of enthusiasm on Viner's part but a measure of acquiescence that is stronger than what Samuelson's retrospective suggests. We reprint the letters here, in their entirety.[18]

October 17, 1930[19]

My dear Dr. Viner:

I am sending you under separate cover a copy of the lectures which you gave in Economics 301 during the summer quarter at the University of Chicago.

I have endeavored to follow your wishes with regard to references to other economists, and I hope that what I have done in this connection will be satisfactory. If I have mis-quoted you at any point, or if there is anything in the lectures which you would like to have changed, I shall be glad to have such changes made in all copies distributed in the future.

I hope that everything is going well with you and that you are having a pleasant year.

Very truly yours,

M.D. Ketchum

Ketchum's letter clearly indicates that Viner had some sense for what Ketchum was up to before he received the notes and that he had impressed some wishes regarding the transcription on him. Although it is impossible to say with certainty what exactly Viner was after here, it may have been a desire to avoid having a written transcription of critical comments about other economists made during the lectures.

Viner replied almost immediately, and his response suggests that he thought that the lectures might actually be of some use to him:

> November 20, 1930
>
> My dear Mr. Ketchum:
>
> Thank you very much for your generosity in sending me a copy of your notes on the lectures which I gave in economics 301 during the last summer course. I am very glad to have them, and I have no doubt that they will contribute to an improvement in the quality of my lectures on subsequent occasions.
>
> Very sincerely yours,

There is no further record of correspondence between them until the spring of 1931, when Ketchum wrote to Viner again, apparently in the hope that Viner might utilize the notes in his course or, at least, allow them to be made available to the students.

> April 21 1931
>
> My dear Dr. Viner,
>
> I understand that you are planning to return to the University of Chicago next year and that you are planning to teach Economics 301 in the Autumn Quarter.
>
> I am wondering if you are going to want to make any use of the mimeographed lectures in this course which you gave during the Summer Quarter of 1930. You may remember that I sent you a copy of these mimeographed lectures some months ago. If you do not want to make any use of these mimeographed lectures as readings, will you have any objection to my letting the class which you teach in the Autumn Quarter know that they are available through me if they want them.
>
> If this is done, are there any changes in the lectures which you would like to have incorporated in any additional copies which I may have mimeographed.
>
> I shall appreciate hearing from you at your convenience.
>
> Very truly yours,
>
> Marshall D. Ketchum

The brevity of Viner's response to Ketchum is perhaps indicative of his uneasiness about the circulation of the notes:

> May 4 1931
>
> My dear Mr. Ketchum:
>
> I do not plan to make any use of your copy of my lectures. What attitude toward them students wish to take is a matter for their decision, with which I do not care to interfere.
>
> Very sincerely yours,

In 1986, Irwin managed to track down the M. D. Ketchum who had edited the notes.[20] Marshall Ketchum reported that he had attended the course in 1930 and that he had been able to take down in shorthand most, but not all, of what Viner said. Other students in the class observed Ketchum's note taking and asked him to make his notes available to others, which presumably explains his query to Viner about their circulation. The notes were typed and soon gained a distribution far beyond the class because of their detail and Viner's reputation. Although Viner and Ketchum had been together at Chicago for some time, Ketchum reports that they never discussed the notes with each other.

Despite their early and wide distribution, the notes seem to have all but disappeared from circulation. The Columbia University Business School library no longer retains a copy of the notes. A copy remains in the stacks at the University of Chicago's Regenstein Library, and a second copy can be found in the George Stigler papers, which are housed in the Special Collections Research Center at the Regenstein Library.[21] Viner's own copy is held in the Viner Papers at Princeton (as are copies of correspondence with Ketchum), and the National Union Catalog of pre-1956 imprints (which is hardly complete) reports that the Library of Congress, Harvard, and Swarthmore also hold copies of the notes. WorldCat reports that the University of Kansas, the University of North Carolina at Chapel Hill, Harvard University, and Cornell University have copies. Still, they should be considered quite rare.

An Overview of the Lectures

According to Samuelson, "[i]n 1935 the course that I took was noticeably different in scope and coverage from the 1930 version."[22] Still, the detailed notes from the 1930 summer class give an indication of what Viner taught. We will not go into great detail here on what the notes reveal, preferring to let them speak for themselves. However, we will briefly summarize them, highlighting certain aspects on occasion. We will not quote from the notes to avoid tying Viner directly to them.[23]

Viner's course was divided into two parts. The first half deals with demand, supply, and industry equilibrium, while the second half covers factor rewards. Viner's opening lecture discusses the characteristics of neoclassical economics and some methodological issues pertaining to economic theory.[24] He says that the course is not a hard one, but that one's conclusions should follow strictly from the assumptions one makes. He then begins with demand analysis, focusing on the utility foundations of demand theory, the elasticity of demand, and the various problems that are associated with estimating demand curves from data. Marshall was the starting point for most of the discussions (In fact, Viner's course led two of his pupils, Milton Friedman and Don Patinkin, to examine Marshall's demand theory in later publications.[25]) In one lecture, Viner suggested that the footnotes and appendices of Marshall contain the most important material, as Marshall succeeded in avoiding precision in the text.

The lectures on cost and supply closely follow the treatment given in his famous 1931 article. Viner clarifies the logic behind the supply curve, using a variety of cost conditions to derive the firm and industry supply curve. In drawing the cost curves, Viner notes that the average variable (or what he calls "direct") cost curve should not begin to be negatively inclined but should be rising throughout. The 1930 lecture was delivered before the Wong-envelope theorem days, and a diagram that was used in the lectures (similar to the famous chart IV in the 1931 article) errs by depicting the long-run average cost curve as running through the minimum points on each short-run average total cost curve.

As in the 1931 article, the distinction between external and internal economies is stressed. Viner also mentions the problems of equilibrium in decreasing cost industries and their tendency toward monopoly. Monopoly is treated in only one lecture, using the usual partial equilibrium diagram; whereas oligopoly (called "partial monopoly") merits only passing mention, because there is no standard graphical exposition. Viner indicates that even monopolies face competitive pressures and are always subject to some price pressure.

Viner devotes two lectures to contrasting Austrian and English value theory. He believes that there would be no issue between the two groups if they could agree on initial assumptions. He has no quarrel with Austrian value theory, given their assumptions, but suggests that the English have the better argument where the two fundamentally disagree. English value theory, however, has been improved by incorporating Austrian elements into it.

The second half of the course deals with payments to factors of production. Attention is devoted primarily to wage and interest theory, with rent and profits briefly discussed at the end of the course. The notes for the second half of the course become more substantial and include Viner's side comments. Perhaps somewhere toward the end of the first half of the course Ketchum was asked by the other students to use his shorthand ability to take more detailed notes for them.

Viner begins with a discussion of the wages-fund theory. He suggests that the theory was never very important as the basis for wage theory, except in analyzing the short-run impact of collective bargaining or sudden increases in the demand for labor. Viner devotes one lecture to Francis Walker's residual-share theory of wages before moving on to the marginal product theory of Clark, whom he chides for claiming an ethical justification for his system of distribution. It is clear, however, that Viner recognizes the importance of the marginal productivity theory.

Viner focuses on three explanations with regard to wage differentials: disutility of certain occupations, Cairnes' noncompeting groups, and the relative bargaining power of labor groups. He provides illustrations of each; for example, gold miners earn more than surface workers because of the unequal disutilities of the tasks. Viner also devotes half a lecture to the problem of income inequality. He says that inequality in Europe is greater than in the United States, but that it is probably increasing in the latter. He discusses arguments about whether inequality is due to nature (ability and IQ) or nurture (environmental factors) without arriving at any definitive conclusions.

With regard to collective bargaining, Viner suggests that the general presumption should be that raising wages lowers the volume of employment, although one could think up reasons as to why this need not hold in the short run. The effect on employment depends mainly on the elasticity of demand for labor. After looking at wage data for union and nonunionized occupations, Viner ventures the opinion that collective bargaining succeeds more in improving working conditions than in increasing the wage rate. The lectures do not discuss the normative aspects of collective bargaining, but rather concentrate on the impact of higher wages on employment and the firm.

One problem that Viner observes with regard to distribution theory is the trap of circular reasoning. Some theorists imply that one factor reward is determined first, and then the others follow as a residual payment. However, how can one be sure that the original factor is not the residual claimant? In other words, if the pattern "a-b-a-b-a-b . . ." is observed, can one determine which precedes the other? According to Viner, one of the important contributions of the Lausanne school is that it avoids circular reasoning by simultaneously solving a system of equations for general equilibrium. He spends time examining Cassel's system of equations and notes that Clark also avoids such problems by simultaneously determining all factor rewards.

Viner then moves on to interest theory. His opening lecture refers to Fisher's recent work in the area as "definitive," and he covers it in later lectures, but starts with Clark's marginal productivity theory of capital. The only diagrams used for this section of the course are the usual downward sloping marginal product curves, with a rectangle indicating the payment to one factor and the triangle under the curve indicating the payment to the other factor. The central problem of interest theory, Viner says, is ascertaining what determines the physical productivity of capital as well as the relationship between capital productivity and interest. He indicates that the ethical basis for the payment of interest is abstinence, whereas the economic basis is that capital is productive. Viner discusses Böhm-Bawerk's approach, Clark on capital versus capital goods, and savings and the supply of capital. In addition, he uses a few numerical examples to illustrate capitalization and discounting, and briefly touches on banking and capital creation.

After all this, Viner has little time to cover rent and profit theory. He challenges the class to find the statement in Ricardo which says that rent does not enter into the cost of production, whereas the remuneration of other factors does. Since he denied that rent entered into marginal cost, Ricardo denied that rent entered into that cost which determines price. Viner uses this example to stress the difference between cost in general and price-determining cost. In a brief discussion of profit theory, Viner refers the class to the work of Knight and Schumpeter.

As one would expect from a Viner course, historical asides are peppered throughout the lectures. For example, he indicates that Turgot may have been the first clear expounder of the law of diminishing returns. While giving due credit to Clark for marginal productivity theory, he indicates that Von Thünen and Longfield had stated this theory earlier. With regard to capital theory, Viner mentions that in his "Interest of Money Examined" (1663), Thomas Manley put forth the idea that the optimal rate at which a forest should be cut down should be determined by the rate of interest and should be such that the rate of forest growth equals the rate of interest. (However, Viner adds that it is quite possible that practical foresters had seen this since time immemorial!) On a broader issue of the history of doctrine, Viner observes that reputations are sometimes more easily made by thinking of a good term for an idea than by discovering an idea.

In his lectures, Viner is not keen on passing final judgment on the theories of others. More frequently, he serves as a guide to contemporary theory, without hesitating to give warnings about pitfalls in the analyses of others. The price theory lectures contain more of Viner's original work. The lectures on distribution basically present and evaluate the theories of other economists by calling attention to differences in approaches and assumptions. The only harsh words to be found in the entire set of notes are reserved for those agricultural economists who are intent on furthering farmers' interests rather than on advancing knowledge through scientific inquiry.

Conclusion

Reading notes taken from lectures cannot capture the excitement and immediacy of live lectures, especially when they are delivered by someone of Viner's quality.[26] Economic theory has been improved and polished since Viner's time: Vinerian cost curves and marginal productivity theory have trickled down to the undergraduates and some topics, such as imperfect competition, are treated in a more systematic manner. However, the range and learning of Viner's knowledge still rings through. The notes make fascinating reading, and historians of economic thought should be grateful that some record of Viner's course survives and provides us with a further insight into the rationale for Samuelson's assessment that "[t]here has never been a greater neoclassical economist than Jacob Viner."[27]

Notes

*   This introduction builds on a paper that was originally prepared by Irwin for the June 1986 History of Economics Society meeting in New York. Without implicating them, Irwin would like to thank Professor Marshall Ketchum for his recollections and Professor Donald Dewey for his encouragement and comments.

1.   In 2011, the Becker Center and the Milton Friedman Institute were merged and became the Becker–Friedman Institute for Research in Economics. See http://news. uchicago.edu/article/2011/06/17/becker-friedman-institute-established-university-chicago. Accessed December 11, 2012.

2.   See Reder (1982), which also contains many references, as well as several of the essays in Emmett (2010) and Van Horn et al. (2011). Medema (2011) discusses the history of Chicago price theory and its relation to the evolution of the study of law and economics at Chicago.

3.   On the continuities and discontinuities in Chicago price theory, see, for example, Reder (1982) and Medema (2011).

4.   Frank Knight's approach to price theory is perhaps best exemplified in *The Economic Organization* (1933). Patinkin (1981, 23–51) summarizes the contents of Knight's Economics 301 course, and a further discussion of Knight's approach can be found in Emmett (2009) and Medema (2011). On Henry Simons, see "The Simons Syllabus," which was edited by Gordon Tullock (1983).

5.   See Knight (1933), Friedman (1962), and Becker (1971).

6.   These were published in 1946, 1952, 1966, and 1987. For an examination of how Chicago price theory evolved in the hands of Friedman and Stigler, see Hammond and Hammond (2006) and Hammond (2010).

7.   One gets a good sense for this from a perusal of Viner's correspondence with his colleagues and university administrators, copies of which can be found in the Jacob Viner papers, which are housed in the Seeley G. Mudd Manuscript Library at Princeton University.

8. On his position in the department and relationship to any "Chicago School," see Patinkin (1981) and Rotwein (1983).
9. Leland, "Jacob Viner: Teacher, Colleague, Friend." Jacob Viner Papers, Box 1, Folder 5, Academic Tributes 1970–1978.
10. See Viner (1931) and the reprint of this article, with a supplementary note, in Viner (1958).
11. See Bloomfield (1992) for an extensive survey of Viner's scholarly contributions.
12. http://www.vanderbilt.edu/AEA/walker_medal.htm. The Walker Medal was discontinued after the creation of the Nobel Memorial Prize in Economics.
13. When asked by Daniel Hammond whether Viner's class had methodological content, Friedman replied: "That depends on what you mean by methodological. It had no explicit methodological content whatsoever. But there was a very strong implicit methodological content, since you came away very clearly with the feeling that you were talking about real problems. Part of the distinction is viewing economics as branch of mathematics—as a game—as in intellectual game and exercise—as Debreu, Arrow, and so on—and it's a fine thing to do. There's nothing wrong with that. After all, mathematics is a perfectly respectable intellectual activity, and so is mathematization of economics or anything else. The other part of it is view it (using Marshall's phrase) as an engine of analysis. And there was no doubt that Viner viewed it as an engine of analysis, and no doubt that when you were in his course that you came away with the feeling that economics really had something to say about real problems and real things. In that sense it had methodological content." Quoted in Hammond (2010, 14).
14. "Introduction to the first Richard T. Ely lecture given by Jacob Viner," Jacob Viner Papers, Box 1, Folder 5, Seeley G. Mudd Manuscript Library, Princeton University, 1962.
15. Ibid.
16. Leland, "Jacob Viner: Teacher, Colleague, Friend."
17. Mitchell, *Types of Economic Theory* (1969). Bearing testimony to Viner's concern about editorial transgressions is a manuscript among his papers at Princeton on which he wrote: "Published; but I have not included it in my bibliography because of unauthorized changes. I accept no responsibility for these changes. J.V." See Machlup (1972, 362). In addition, see Patinkin (1981, 267).
18. These letters can be found in the Jacob Viner Papers, Box 35, Folder 20, "General, 1917–1940," Seeley G. Mudd Manuscript Library, Princeton University.
19. These letters were sent to Viner while he was at the Institute Universitaire de Hautes Etudes Internationales in Geneva.
20. Marshall D. Ketchum earned his Ph.D. at the University of Chicago and, after stints at Duke University, Utah State University, and the University of Kentucky, he was professor of Finance at the University of Chicago's Graduate School of Business from 1946 to 1971. He was the president of the American Finance Association in 1957 and served as editor of the *Journal of Finance* from 1946 to 1955. He passed away in 1989.
21. Ketchum informed Irwin that he himself no longer had a copy of the notes.
22. For example, the discussion of the concept of equilibrium by analogy to a well-balanced aquarium, cited by Samuelson (1972, 7) as one of the most memorable elements of the course, occurred in the last of the lectures from 1930; whereas it was, according to Samuelson, discussed in the first lecture of 1935. Samuelson also makes reference to this analogy in a letter to Viner on April 9, 1948 (Viner Papers, Box 23, Folder 11, Seeley G. Mudd Manuscript Library, Princeton University).

23. See Note 7. One should be careful not to misrepresent Viner's views as they might appear in the lecture notes. The context of the discussion is vitally important. If Viner appears to make a statement on some issue, he may just be expressing views held by others rather than asserting something on his own.
24. In discussing the characteristics of neoclassical economics, Viner notes that it places relatively little emphasis on consumption. This bears importance to questions surrounding Viner's customs-union theory and lends support to Michaely's (1976) conclusion that Viner overlooked consumption effects which could make a trade-diverting union welfare improving.
25. Perhaps the most controversial of these student treatments of Marshall is Friedman's article on "The Marshallian Demand Curve," in which Friedman attempts to make the case that Marshall posited a purchasing-power-constant (Hicksian) demand curve. Viner's correspondence with Friedman from the 1940s suggests that he (unlike many others) approved of Friedman's interpretation of Marshall.
26. One gets a similar feeling while reading the history of economic thought lectures of Viner's dear friend, Lionel Robbins. The printed version of the lectures makes for an exceptionally good read, but they cannot fully capture the magisterial nature of Robbins' delivery that one finds in the audio tapes of the lectures. See Robbins (1998).
27. Samuelson (1972, 9). All quotes are from his 1972 article; see also his "Economics in a Golden Age: A Personal Memoir" (1983).

References

Baumol, William J. 1972. "Jacob Viner at Princeton." *Journal of Political Economy* 80 (January/February): 12–15.

Becker, Gary S. 1971. *Economic Theory.* New York: McGraw-Hill. Transaction ed., 2007.

Bloomfield, Arthur I. 1992. "On the Centenary of Jacob Viner's Birth: A Retrospective View of the Man and His Work." *Journal of Economic Literature* 30 (December): 2052–85.

Breit, William, and Barry T. Hirsch. 2009. *Lives of the Laureates: Twenty-Three Nobel Economists.* 5th ed. Cambridge: MIT Press.

Bronfenbrenner, Martin. 1982. "On the Superlative in Samuelson." In *Samuelson and Neoclassical Economics,* ed. George R. Feiwell. Boston, MA: Kluwer-Nijhoff Publishers, 345–56.

Emmett, Ross. 2009. *Frank Knight and the Chicago School in American Economics.* London: Routledge.

———. 2010. *The Elgar Companion to the Chicago School of Economics.* Cheltenham: Edward Elgar Publishing.

———. 2011. "Sharpening Tools in the Workshop: The Workshop System and the Chicago School's Success." In *Building Chicago Economics: New Perspectives on the History of America's Most Powerful Economics Program,* ed. Robert Van Horn, Philip Mirowski, and Thomas A. Stapleford. New York: Cambridge University Press, 93–115.

Friedman, Milton. 1962. *Price Theory: A Provisional Text.* Chicago, IL: Aldine. 2nd ed., 1976. Transaction ed., 2007.

Hammond, J. Daniel. 2010. "The Development of Post-War Chicago Price Theory." In *The Elgar Companion to the Chicago School of Economics,* ed. Ross B. Emmett. Northampton, MA: Edward Elgar, 7–24.

Hammond, J. Daniel, and Claire H. Hammond, eds. 2006. *Making Chicago Price Theory: Friedman-Stigler Correspondence, 1945–1957.* New York: Routledge.

Ketchum, M. D., ed. 1930. *Lectures in Economics 301 (Price and Distribution Theory)*. Chicago, IL.

Knight, Frank H. 1933. *The Economic Organization*. Mimeo, University of Chicago. Repr. New York: A. Kelley, 1957.

Levitt, Steven D., and Stephen J. Dubner. 2005. *Freakonomics: A Rogue Economist Explores the Hidden Side of Everything*. New York: William Morrow.

Machlup, Fritz. 1972a. "What the World Thought of Jacob Viner." *Journal of Political Economy* 80 (January/February): 1–4.

———. 1972b. "What Was Left on Viner's Desk." *Journal of Political Economy* 80 (March/April): 353–64.

Medema, Steven G. 2011. "Chicago Price Theory and Chicago Law and Economics: A Tale of Two Transitions." In *Building Chicago Economics: New Perspectives on the History of America's Most Powerful Economics Program*, ed. Robert Van Horn, Philip Mirowski, and Thomas Stapleford. New York: Cambridge University Press, 151–79.

Michaely, M. 1976. "The Assumptions of Jacob Viner's Theory of Customs Unions." *Journal of International Economics* 6 (February): 75–93.

Mitchell, Wesley C. 1969. *Types of Economic Theory*. 2 vols. New York: Augustus M. Kelley.

Patinkin, Don. 1981. *Essays On and In the Chicago Tradition*. Durham, NC: Duke University Press.

Reder, Melvin. 1982. "Chicago Economics: Permanence and Change." *Journal of Economic Literature* 20 (March): 1–38.

Robbins, Lionel. 1998. *A History of Economic Thought: The LSE Lectures*, ed. Steven G. Medema and Warren J. Samuels. Princeton, NJ: Princeton University Press.

Rotwein, Eugene. 1983. "Jacob Viner and the Chicago Tradition." *History of Political Economy* 15 (Summer): 265–80.

Samuelson, Paul A. 1972. "Jacob Viner, 1892-1970." *Journal of Political Economy* 80 (January–February): 5–11.

———. 1983. "Economics in a Golden Age: A Personal Memoir." In *Paul Samuelson and Modern Economic Theory*, ed. E. Cary Brown and Robert M. Solow. New York: McGraw-Hill, 1–14.

Stigler, George J. 1942. *The Theory of Competitive Price*. New York: Macmillan.

———. 1946. *The Theory of Price*. New York: Macmillan. 2nd ed., 1952; 3rd ed., 1966; 4th ed., 1988.

———. 1988. *Memoirs of an Unregulated Economist*. New York: Basic Books.

Tullock, Gordon, ed. 1983. *The Simons Syllabus*. Fairfax, VA: Center for the Study of Public Choice, George Mason University.

Viner, Jacob. 1931. "Cost Curves and Supply Curves." *Zeitschrift für Nationalokonomie* 3 (September): 23–46. Repr. with the supplementary note in *The Long View and the Short*. Glencoe, IL: The Free Press, 1958, 50–84.

———. 1958. *The Long View and the Short*. Glencoe, IL: The Free Press.

Part I

Lectures in Economics 301

First Term

June 17, 1930

Neoclassical economics is a sympathetic evolution of the English Classical School. Included under neoclassical economics is the English–American version in Taussig and Marshall and also the Austrian school, whose differences are not as important as the resemblances to the Anglo–American type. Included also is the Continental Equilibrium School or the Mathematical School, such as Walras, Pareto, and their followers. They have much more in common with the neoclassicists than in dispute.

Neoclassical economics is deductive or a priori in its method. It is static. It does not discuss laws of change, but it discusses processes of equilibrium under given circumstances. It takes value as its central problem and approaches economic problems in value terms, meaning exchange value. It discusses ratios of exchange between commodities and prices in the relative, not the absolute, aspect. It puts little emphasis on consumption. It puts no emphasis on institutional influences on prices and distribution. It does not explore the origin of value. It has both price economics and welfare economics phases. It is an objective description of the process of price determination under certain assumed conditions. It is also an appraisal of price-determination processes. It is, therefore, a welfare economics. The main emphasis is on a descriptive, objective explanation of the way in which prices come to be what they are.

It is qualitative rather than quantitative. "Qualitative" refers to "measure." Neoclassical economics has very little to do with arithmetical measurements, but it deals with quantities, primarily in terms of more or less. An increase in demand means an increase in price; it does not tell us how much of an increase.

It says that two things may be equal but it does not tell us how much each quantity must be. It is not quantitative in the narrow, technical sense, because it does not measure quantities. It indicates rank of size rather than indicating relative size. This system indicates rank in terms of A, B, C, D, and E, rather than in terms of 1, 2, 3, 4, and 5. It is not known how much larger E is than A. Neoclassical economics states inequalities in terms of greater or less.

This is to be a course in syllogistic logic. It is not concerned particularly with the validity of the premises nor the method as a whole, nor with the adequacy or significance of the conclusions or the validity of the conclusions. It is a course in technique, and almost that alone. It is concerned with internal validity. The course consists of tests of sound economic reasoning. The course is intended to train you in the essential logical tools in classical and neoclassical economics.

I am going to hold you rigidly to the premises with which you start. You may reach erroneous conclusions, but they must be the necessary outcome from the erroneous premises from which you start. Your conclusions must be consistent with your premises. You must use the tools of economics accurately and quickly. When you define a term, you must use it the way you define it. You must be consistent in your terminology. Your conclusions must have some relationship to your premises. You have undoubtedly certain accumulated bad mental habits of which you must rid yourself. There are only a few principles in the course; it is not a hard course.

We shall use the law of diminishing utility very little. The technological laws of return are studied, and certain other phenomena called the laws of cost or the "trends of cost" are studied, as well as certain assumptions as to the way in which business man operate, the way they react to certain phenomena when operating in the market place.

Classical and neoclassical economics has been subjected to vigorous criticism. The criticism has been that classical economics has gotten into an academic mood which does not have any relation to actual problems. The fact that value theory has become an academic discipline in which it is taught has given it a sort of value and existence of its own apart from its relationship to actual phenomena. The classical and neo-classical type of economics in the hands of an amateur is very dangerous.

Part of the difficulty in finding a satisfactory economic method is due to the difficulty of the economic problem. By their very nature, economic problems present the scientist with a more serious test of his technique, I think, than does any other field of human knowledge. There are parallels, but they are not in physics, which is a simple thing compared to economics. In the medical fields, parallels can be found. There are two great difficulties in the economic problem:

1. They involve many variables in a way which is not true in physics, in astronomy, etc. The probability theory rests on the assumption that there shall be many variables in the situation. This theory requires that it shall be possible to reduce the phenomena to homogeneous phenomena. The phenomena must be of the same order. The myriad variables must be of coordinate importance. Every phenomenon is the product of many variables but many are of insignificant importance in economic analysis. The variables must be of coordinate rank.
2. In most of the physical sciences, the scientist does not err greatly if he assumes that at the beginning and end of his period of observations, processes do not change much. The laboratory scientist artificially creates a situation in which he can free himself from worry by deliberate experimentation and artificial control. He keeps other things constant. In economics we cannot do this. Much importance must be attached to the fact that the economist relies on observation of phenomena in an uncontrolled world; elements of flux are so much more important in his case than in the physical and natural sciences. Things change so much more rapidly in economics. In the medical sciences, for many purposes, the scientist would not expect to find very much qualification, because his study of a physiological process was made in the year 1930 instead of in 1900. He can find out these processes, if he wants to find them out, from an animal lower than man.

For the economist this is not true. There is one type of attack against neo-classical economics which exaggerates the extent to which this is not true. This type of attack puts much emphasis on the change that economic processes undergo and states that these processes change at least every decade. There is no tangible evidence that the mode of operation of the businessman in the wholesale market is different in any fundamental respect today from what it was in 1600. There has not been any fundamental change in trading between professional traders. There are important differences today between the attitude and types of reactions of the household buyer and the operations of a wholesale buyer for a wholesale concern. There is a great difference between the layman and the professional. These differences are of substantial importance. Most of the time, the neoclassical economist is discussing wholesale markets.

The labor market is a retail market, so far as the seller is concerned. When there is collective bargaining, a certain amount of professionalism is introduced on the selling side. On the buying side, there is a good deal of professionalism.

These difficulties, the multitude of factors in the situation, the fact that they are not of coordinate importance so that the scope for the probability theory is very limited, the fact that there is much more flux than in the natural sciences, the fact that the method of experiment is closed so that we cannot fix that flux, these factors result in requiring analysis of the economic method of inquiry. The isolation of the factors conceptually requires the use of "other things being equal," or the development of some empirical, rational method of analysis of actual economic phenomena.

Actual economic phenomena divide themselves into two groups. It is possible to find regional areas, or you may get comparable data in another way produced by different moments in time.

In finding regional areas, it is necessary to reduce the various regions to homogeneity. For time series, there is the problem of the change through time. The systematic, inductive methods, largely statistical, have largely been confined to the historical, regional, comparative studies. Very great difficulties are involved. Without arguing for the logical, intellectually satisfactory character of the neoclassical technique in many respects, it is at least a possibility where we have not yet learned how to deal scientifically with historical series. We do not know how to get the irregularities out of historical data. Very little has been done in the study of regionally comparable data in economics. Accounting for regional differences has not been seriously thought of.

The neoclassical method is a primitive method. It is not the only method available. The task of developing for economics with its complications and special difficulties, techniques comparable in their intellectual equality to the technique of the laboratories is still a task to be accomplished. In the meantime over a wide area, the only method we have for reaching conclusions is the method of deductive analysis. A lot of statistical work done has been historical. It tells you that such and such things happened at such and such a time. Ninety percent of economic statistical analysis has not been analysis but has given a summarized, abbreviated statement of what happened at a certain time. People have thought that it was analysis when it was not.

Statistical theory has moved much farther in the last twenty-five years. However, we have accepted as discovered things which would to the physical sciences seem like questions. Problems of verification have been more difficult in economics. Standards in economics are at least as high as those of the physician. There are certain degrees of plausibility attached to the economist's theories, but so there is with what the physician regards as hypotheses. A good many social scientists, those who have become acquainted with the standards and requirements of laboratory technique, have developed an overpowering inferiority complex. There is not any occasion for this. They can recognize that in terms of degrees of probability, they stand in the lower rank. This is not due to the fact that the social scientist has lower intelligence. The social scientist is attacking more difficult problems. The social scientist should recognize that his methods are primitive, not due to his incompetence, but to the difficulties of the problem. Mankind has not as yet found out how to develop a high-grade technique. Economics is not alone in this difficulty. Some of the social sciences are in a worse position. The scientific student of blood faces a situation comparable in some degree. In economic problems, the mathematical technique breaks down. It is impossible to actually analyze in mathematical terms when the number of equations gets to be very great. Economics requires many equations.

June 18, 1930

The law of diminishing utility as a psychological law is old and dates back to the seventeenth century. It was used for what we call "welfare analysis" in the eighteenth century. It got into economics with Lloyd's essay on the theory of value in 1834.[1] It did not get into economics to any great extent until Jevons introduced it in England and Walras in France and Menger in Austria about simultaneously. It is a psychological law; it is a statement as to the consequences of the acquisition of successive units of a commodity of the same kind.

For an explanation of price determination, it is rationalistic hedonism. That sort of psychology is supposed to be very much out of date. Economists must be on their guard that they do not state that men rationally base their buying decisions on rationalism. The psychologists say that men do not eat because they have previously come to the conclusion that if they did eat they would derive certain satisfactions therefrom; they eat simply because they are hungry.

Bentham and Mill brought in hedonism, and they are the pronounced hedonists. The hedonistic philosophers did not care to apply the utility theory to economic price theory. The men who would throw out utility theory can state their propositions in terms which would have been unavailable to them if utility analysis had not shown the way. Water is more useful than diamonds and yet diamonds are more valuable than water. This ceases to be a problem once utility analysis is introduced. All that economics needs to assert is that men will desire additional units less than they desired the preceding ones. Economics needs a law of diminishing utility as a law of diminishing desire. Whether the law of diminishing desire is a rational consequence or whether it is a primary factor does not make any difference at all to an economist as a price theorist.

The psychologists have not been enthusiastic about the economic law of diminishing utility. They tend to attribute it to a misreading of the so-called "Weber–Fechner law" in psychology. The stimulus is the dependent variable in this law. The law is that it takes an increasing stimulus to bring out a constant reaction. Some psychologists state that there is a law of diminishing satisfaction corresponding to a law of diminishing sensation, but most of them do not say anything about this.

The uniformity of five matched pearls gives the five pearls an added value. This adds to the price. Most of the criticisms of the diminishing utility theory would be irrelevant to diminishing utility in terms of desire only. Criticisms which have been made on grounds of hedonistic taint would not hold against a statement in this form.

Another line of objection against the theory is that there is no sense in dealing with something beyond the capacity of direct measurement. It is impossible to measure it, and, therefore, it is absurd to make quantitative statements. However, I can cite certain necessary equalities without telling you the sizes of the terms. I can also tell you about the order of size under certain circumstances. We can posit necessary equalities and can tell something about the order of size.

$$P_a : P_b :: MU_a : MU_b$$

The price of commodity a is to the price of commodity b as the marginal utility of commodity a is to the marginal utility of commodity b.

June 19, 1930

It is said against utility economics that what the economist wants is demand schedules. Utility schedules can be known by inference only from demand schedules. This is the claim of the opponents. There is this basis for insisting upon the differentiation and separate existence of utility schedules and demand schedules:

1. Appeal to introspection. Introspection has lost its responsibility as a main source of information for the psychologist. One cannot depend too much on introspection. There is the analogy from the Weber–Fechner law. Psychologists do not know how to test the law of diminishing desire the way they have tested the law of diminishing reaction.
2. If we were guided by laws of diminishing desire, it would lead to the moral economy, an efficient management of our behavior. It would lead to a prudential or rational system of life.

The law of diminishing desire or utility is a hypothesis. We contingently assert the existence of such a law, because if it did exist, it would explain wide ranges of phenomena. It serves to explain and relate to each other the negative demand schedules. It is necessary to explain negative slope of demand schedules in terms of psychological reactions to a stimulus of the same kind. "Desire" does not necessarily mean "consciousness." It does not assert that we know that we want the second less than the first. It is possible to have an unconscious desire. Consciousness is a marginal phenomenon. Psychologists have borrowed from the utility theory certain concepts and tools and certain ways of arranging their findings. In the Austrian school of value, there is one school in philosophy and one school in economics. Meinong-Ehrenfels took the concepts that Menger worked out and applied them to behavior with the rationalism taken out. At the margin where there is equal balancing, consciousness is called upon to decide. It is only when the two alternatives are closely balanced that there is any virtue for rational behavior in being rational, in thinking and calculating. Under any other circumstances, that is not necessary in order that you shall act in a way which shall not bring disaster later on.

Meinong-Ehrenfels has changed the terminology of "psychology." He speaks of the law of the threshold of consciousness where rational decision requires a careful survey of the factors involved. Below that he speaks of two levels, one of which is the hedonic level. Wordsworth has been willing to lay down the existence, for desires and for feelings, of a law like the Weber–Fechner law. This law applies not only to physical sensations but to feelings. No economist need feel concerned lest the psychologist would laugh at him if he holds to a tentative adherence to a theory, as yet not completely verified, of a law of diminishing utility.

Satisfactions cannot exert influence directly in the market place. The stage at which they would work would be a rationalistic stage. You might mold and develop your desires, getting into action through price offers. There is a conceivable and possible wide range of discrepancies between the phenomena of satisfaction and the phenomena of desire and their objective manifestations in the form of price offers, etc.

For our purposes, we do not need to go back to satisfactions. In welfare economics, it is necessary to use care in identifying desire with satisfaction. The desire that works is always a short-run desire. But for welfare analysis, one should think that the satisfaction which enters into the calculus should be the long-run satisfaction.

I am going to expect you to become an expert in distinguishing demand schedules and utility schedules. Marshall does this, although there is no genuine utility analysis in Marshall. There is also none in Taussig. There are not many writers in the American or English school who have not confused utility schedules with demand schedules and price analysis. Edgeworth has been the leading exponent of a genuine utility analysis. It is seen the earliest in his *Mathematical Psychics*. In this country, Irving Fisher's *Mathematical Investigations in the Theory of Value and Prices* is important. All of Davenport's writings are also important, particularly his *Value and Distribution*. These, together with Wicksteed, the English economist, are the only American and English economists who have succeeded in distinguishing utility analysis from price analysis.[2]

An explanation of the relationship between marginal utility and price is found in Irving Fisher's *Mathematical Investigations* and Edgeworth's *Mathematical Psychics*.

Demand is a fundamental concept of neoclassical economics. There is, however, no place for the concept of ineffective demand. The quantity taken is not the definition of demand. A change of price is already in a concept of demand. Quantity taken is a function of price. The word "demand" has other meanings in nontechnical usage. Many economists speak of the demand falling off if the price falls. Very few economists have succeeded in avoiding ambiguity in that connection. There is this natural tendency because of the conflict between the technical use of the term and the ordinary business use of the term. Confusion in the two meanings often leads to a plausible error. There is a reduction in the quantity taken and not a reduction in demand.

When you are defining demand, what price do you use? If there is an actually existing schedule at any one time, it can be true only to a certain limited extent. If there is an existing schedule, it is a schedule within a very narrow range of the common experience. It is a statement of the amounts that would be taken if the price were such and such. It is regarded as a forecast of what people would do without implying that they know what they would do or what they are going to do. A demand schedule is conceptual. If you are talking of a market demand schedule or the momentary demand schedule, you are asserting something about the response which people would make to the actual market prices You may be speaking of a price which would never occur. Such forecasts are likely to be dangerous. Ordinarily, almost universally, economists lay down the proposition that the demand schedule must have a negative inclination. Drawn graphically, it is said that the demand schedule must slope downward and to the right.

Diamonds may be cheaper at a high price than at a low price in terms of what you are willing to pay, because you are buying expensiveness. A high price makes the diamonds more attractive to you per carat. A change in price in this case will affect the nature of the unit. A potato famine in Ireland means a high price for potatoes and a low real income for the Irish. It is said that the English workers eat more bread when it is high in price. The baking industry in this country is good in depression years.

June 20, 1930

We will assume for the sake of simplicity that all demand curves are negative. There is the theoretical possibility the demand curves may sometimes be positively inclined.

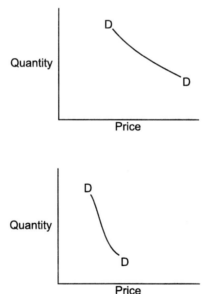

This is not an attempt to be precise. Any writer who gives you charts of this sort is not trying to tell any more than the minimum that he can tell with certainty. A curve like the above tells you that the demand curve slopes negatively and to the right. No. (1) of these curves is the more elastic.

The concept of elasticity was laid down by Cournot.[3] Unit elasticity: As price increases, the amount taken decreases so that the total is the same. You approach to a description of the constant outlay curve if you speak of small changes, and therefore, you will find that Marshall never says that a 50 percent increase in price will bring about a 50 percent decrease in the amount taken.

For finite quantities, there is a discrepancy and the discrepancy grows larger the higher you go in numbers. Unit elasticity is approximately explained by the proposition that a small increase in price will bring about a proportionate decrease in the quantity taken.

A has a more elastic demand than B if a given relative increase in price brings about a greater relative decrease in the amount taken. You cannot tell unless you get price changes and quantity changes in relative form. In order to know which curve is more elastic, it is necessary to know the scales on the axes. If the scales are the same, it is possible to compare them. Without knowing the axes, you cannot tell just simply by inspection whether the curve is elastic or inelastic.

A good deal of the most important matter in Marshall is in the footnotes and appendices. Appendix H is very important. Marshall succeeded in avoiding precision in his text. When he is actually precise, he gives the material in his appendices.

You should have at your fingertips two or three formulae for the elasticity of demand.

The constant outlay curve is a curve with the constant elasticity of 1.

The formula for constant elasticity is $xy^n = c$ (constant amount). A unit elasticity curve is a curve in which the power is one.

One sometimes finds stable demand. That usually means a demand curve which does not shift to any great extent. The stability is in the quantity taken, the price remaining the same over a period of time. There would be a stable demand curve if there were not much change in demand. It is often said that the demand for necessaries is inelastic. We are in the pioneer stage in learning about demand curves. In the case of several things that we think of as necessaries, if they were absolute necessaries, and if we were to draw a demand curve for them, the point about the first unit would have to represent all that one could possibly realize from his resources. There would be an inelastic demand except for this factor: If we start from zero with absolute necessities, then in the early stages of the curve, there must be a very high degree of elasticity, because one is offering everything he has for a first unit. One can offer only the same for the first plus a second unit.

With an elasticity of less than one, the total amount spent decreases with an increase in the quantities offered in return for that amount. With an elasticity of less than unity, the lower the price the less the total amount spent. When the demand is inelastic, the larger the amount offered for sale, the smaller amount one is willing to pay for that aggregate stock.

To measure elasticity, draw logarithms on a natural scale chart and if there is constant elasticity, the result will be a straight line. Then, secure the rate of slope of this line.

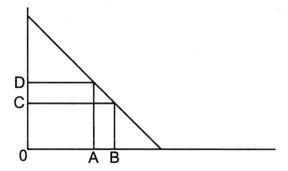

In the above diagram the ratio of CD to AB is the measure of the elasticity. You may secure a straight line on logarithmic paper or on natural scale paper if you are using logarithms.

$$\frac{d \log x}{d \log y} \quad \text{or} \quad \frac{\Delta \log x}{\Delta \log y}$$

The English demand for American wheat is one demand as the farmer in Idaho sees it and another demand as the buyer in Liverpool sees it. The demand of the Liverpool grain importer for American wheat may be quite elastic, while the Idaho farmer would find the demand quite inelastic. How is it possible to derive the demand for wheat on the farm from the demand for wheat at Liverpool? You must be able to subtract the freight rate from the English demand price and then, you would get the demand as the Idaho producer sees it. In the process of deriving it, what might be an elastic demand at Liverpool might be a very inelastic demand for the Idaho producer.

Suppose you are asked to get a demand curve from price and quantity data as they are available under ordinary market conditions:

	Price	Quantity
1910	$10	1000
1911	12	1100
1912	10	950
1913	10	1050

Marshall would not accept this as proof that the demand schedule has shifted, because when he discusses a demand schedule he assumes that the price level remains constant. If the demand schedule had not shifted, the quantity of 950 might be changed to 1,000 or the price would be changed so that the amounts would be consistent with a negative demand schedule.

The method of obtaining the average might limit the use of this demand schedule. For instance,

1,000 units might be sold at $5 in one month, and
2,000 units might be sold at $3 in one month.

What price do you want to use? Should the figures be converted to the amount sold per day? It is necessary to know at what price a quantity of 3,000 would be sold. It is a very complicated problem. If there is constant elasticity, one should use a weighted average and it would have to be averaged by harmonic means.

Where storing is possible, and when the price is $3 and the wholesaler expects the price to rise to $5, the wholesaler will store the grain. This, however, has little bearing on the demand schedule. If during the early part of a month when the price was $5, it was the general belief that the price was going to rise to $6 or $7, buyers might buy to store for the future and may anticipate a future demand schedule. In this case, anticipations as to future prices come into the situation. Where storing is possible, calculations in the market are affected not merely by the demand schedule in a given unit of time, but also by the possibility of buying now to meet the demand of a future time. Under those circumstances, it is possible to get data quite consistent with a negative demand schedule.

It is necessary to understand this implicit assumption in Marshall and that is that *OM* in the diagram below represents the quantity of the commodity that would be taken in the unit period if the price remained *ON* and there were no expectations as to future prices.

The problem of risk may lead to different behavior according to what the attitude toward risk is. Assuming that risk is not taken into consideration, you get the same results for a Marshallian demand curve if it is interpreted with the price *ON* continuing through the unit period. *ON* will take that price providing people think that prices are going to continue into the succeeding period.

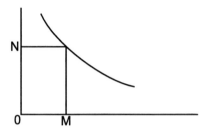

Here is another complication. Suppose that buyers would buy at the rate *OM* if the price remains at *ON*. Suppose the commodity is wheat. At a price *ON*, *OM* units will be bought if the price of barley is 50¢. In Marshall's assumptions, prices of other commodities must remain the same. It is possible to change the price level and yet maintain relative prices the same.

Marshall's concept of demand is that $Q_a = F(P_a)$ (The quantity of commodity *a* is a function of the price of *a*.). There is an infinite number of combinations of other prices, and there is an infinite number of commodities that could be sold at one time at a price of $1.00 per bushel because of different prices for other things.

The Continental Mathematical school generalized this concept of demand as follows:

$$Qu_a = F(P_a, P_b, \cdots \quad \cdots \quad \cdots \quad P_n)$$ (Walras)

$$Qu_a = F(P_a, P_b, \cdots \quad \cdots \quad \cdots \quad P_n, P_T, P_K, P_L)$$ (Pareto)

(In the last formula, $T =$ Land, $K =$ Capital, and $L =$ Labor.)

The quantity of wheat that would be bought for $1.00 per bushel depends on almost everything else. It cannot logically be said that Marshall is right in saying "other things being equal," because they cannot remain equal. This is not the same as static economics. A change in the price of *a* will cause changes in the price of *b* and other commodities. The Marshallian method is logically not legitimate.

It is impossible to draw a real demand schedule on a two-dimensional chart. What is the defense for the Marshallian technique? He might answer that the prices of many other factors are not significant. He would answer: "Let us hope that they are not significant. If they are significant, they are too complex to be used." If these other factors are not significant, the Marshallian method hopes that to the extent that it is logically invalid, the error shall not produce serious practical consequences.

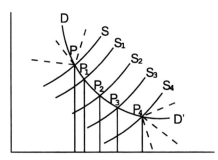

Suppose you are trying to derive an actual demand curve from actual price and quantity sold data. There is the possibility of using regional data where everything is the same in each district except the price. But, this condition is hard to find, where regions are different, including the price, and where it is assumed that all other things are irrelevant or offset each other. What is the relationship of quantity taken per capita between different regions to the price? It is hard to find satisfactory commodities which can be dealt with in that way. Street car fares and transportation may be dealt with in this way, in terms of the number of rides per 1,000 of population and in terms of the rate charged per trip. Getting a Marshallian demand curve out of price and quantity data is very difficult.

June 25, 1930

Suppose that in five years you have five quantities sold during these years. The problem of averaging raises an issue. Suppose that in each year prices remained unaltered during the year and that there are no problems of carryover and no problems of anticipation of future price. It is not necessary that they shall be successive years. Let us assume, however, that this was their chronological order. The supply curve is shifting to the right annually, and the demand remains constant throughout the period. The data would be a series of five prices and a series of quantities joining the points. All probability propositions in economics ought to be considered with a serious amount of hesitation. Probability is a substitute for information. The five points can be joined in a great number of ways. Without resort to probability theory, you would not know how to join the five points.

This is a much more favorable situation than you can ever get out of actual data.

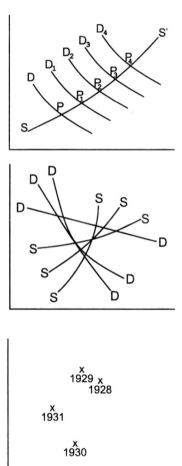

Supposing you had four points and the quantities taken during the years at those points and I should ask you to get a demand curve, as in the foregoing diagram. Supplies and demands have been changing from year to year and from such, it is desired to get a demand schedule. Some things can be done with the possibility of a high degree of error. You may work on the basis of per capita trend. You might assume that the demand curve has been shifting to the right at the same rate as population has been increasing. This gives a clue as to the change in the position of the demand curve. Actually, there is an infinite number of demand schedules that can be derived out of a situation like this. It is hopeless to try to get a Marshallian demand curve out of a situation like this. It is possible to get a good enough proximation to the demand schedule when one or the other is fairly stable. If they are both shifting, it is not legitimate to assume that one is relatively stable. In order to find a satisfactory Marshallian demand schedule out of price and quantity data ordinarily available to us, we have still a long way to go. Schultz is working on the short-run deviations from trends.

Demand curves change from year to year, but they move backward and forward rather than generally forward. In working with such data, there are probably psychical and seasonal trends in the demand schedules. If you are working with annual data, you are working with average prices and total quantities sold, and you may be working with something which does not have much meaning. You may get data for the summer season and for the winter season. Every time you think of another possibility, you think of another difficulty of getting a Marshallian demand schedule out of statistical data.

The dynamic demand schedule is of no significance whatsoever except as history, but that this is a matter of temperamental attitude. It might be possible to find the Marshallian demand curve for each year. Assuming that what you want to do is to forecast the price or volume of sales, you would have to do the same thing for supply. If you could forecast the Marshallian demand and Marshallian supply curve, you would have a more accurate basis for forecasting price. We do not yet know how to perform this task satisfactorily.

Wesley Mitchell has suggested that the Marshallian demand curve is not useful. As economics is getting more quantitative and more scientific, it is finding that these historical demand propositions are becoming more useful. The Marshallian demand curve is the ultimate goal of most investigators. Marshall's demand curve is expressed by the formula $Qu_a = F(P_a)$.

According to the Continental Mathematical school, the quantity is a function of the prices of all commodities. It is obvious that one cannot work with this formula $Qu_a = F(P_a, P_b, \cdots \ \cdots \ \cdots \ \cdots \ P_n)$.

It is possible, however, to pick out the most important of the items. Mordecai Ezekiel has applied multiple correlation to this problem and has taken five or six items for study. Conceivably, if you are working with wheat, you could find out what are the four or five commodities whose prices are most significant to the buyer of wheat. It is possible to find which are the substitutes or rival commodities for wheat.

Some of the statisticians argue that you can account for almost all the variation in the quantity taken of a commodity by relating it to multiple correlation through four or five items. The chief contribution of the statistical work of Moore, Schultz, etc. to demand analysis has been that they have forced the a priori theorists to state their theories more accurately and with more precision.[4] They have not stated their theories more precisely than Marshall, but Marshall is exceptional in that regard. On one point, Marshall was not explicit—here he would have been if he had tried to get a statistical demand curve, and that is that Marshall does not point out clearly enough that the relative prices of other things are assumed to remain constant. Therefore, his demand curve is relative to the particular distribution of other prices at that moment.

Does Marshall ever say that these other things must should remain the same, and does the original level at which they remain the same help to determine what the demand curve shall be? There is a question as to whether he was sufficiently explicit on this point.

There is one type of proposition which it is a good thing to remember. A partial demand curve tends always to be highly elastic. The demand of England for American wheat is likely to be highly elastic. The demand of any country for a particular product from another country is likely to be highly elastic. Let the American price change from the world price and there will be a substantial change in the amount of American wheat which England will take. In the same way, export supplies of a particular country in international trade are likely to be elastic, even though the supply as a whole may be highly inelastic. The amount you are willing to sell abroad will fall very sharply if the foreign price falls below the domestic price even slightly.

It is possible for the demand to be elastic in terms of price delivered, yet it may seem very inelastic at the factory as the producer sees it, if in between the producer and the consumer there is an inflexible transportation or duty cost.

Supposing there are two rival commodities, beef and pork, there are three alternatives when the price of beef changes. When the price of beef rises, (1) the price of pork may remain the same; (2) the price of pork may rise; and (3) the price of pork may fall. The consumption of beef will fall off most when the price of pork falls. Suppose the price of beef falls and the price of pork rises, and then the consumption of beef will be increased. If the price of beef and pork vary directly, it may be still true that when beef goes up, there may be a shift to the consumption of pork even when pork goes up to the same extent. This would be an economy measure.

June 26, 1930

I shall now assume that you know what a demand curve and a supply curve are. We shall now proceed from the schedule concept to one which is more primitive.

There are competitive markets in which the price can remain unaltered for a month. The organization of the market may be such that the price could be too high for equilibrium purposes. There is a price carryover from the previous day. The question is, how shall the existing price be changed, or shall it be changed? Offers to buy are tendencies to push the price up. It is probably a more realistic way of thinking of price to think of it as a sort of pushball. The question of where it shall move is a question of the relative strength of these sets of forces. It is very rare that there is a situation in which the actual price is an equilibrium price in the Marshallian sense. The price could go on for thirty years without having once reached equilibrium. Equilibrium ordinarily will never be reached.

Suppose you have at any one time a price which is approximately an equilibrium price. The evidence would be that it can continue without obvious signs of discomfiture on the part of buyers or sellers. Let us assume that it is an equilibrium price, a price at which the rate of output would be equal to the rate of purchase at which the buyers would be willing to engage it at that price. It is not the price at which purchases equal sales. One cannot speak of the supply price. Any point on the supply schedule is a supply price. The equilibrium price is the price at which the two rates are the same, the rate of willingness to buy and the rate of willingness to sell. The long-run rate is the rate at which potential consumers are willing to use, equaling the rate at which the producers are willing to produce.

Does market value exaggerate the value of capital stock? If you assume this, you assume that the present holders of the stock are out of the demand. They are part of the prevailing demand and are a part of the demand for the stock.

It is said by some that the fact that present holders would not sell at the prevailing prices minimizes the value of the stock. This is a more valid argument. Those holders who have a reserve price higher than the market price are putting a higher value on their stock, and, therefore, the value of the stock is likely to be higher than the value per unit times the number of units. There are cases where a fraction of the stock may be worth more than the same fraction of the aggregate value of the stock as a whole. The remaining fraction that needs to be acquired in order to have a complete unit or voting control may have much greater value to the individuals than the aliquot portion that they would be able to pay for all of the shares.

We are dealing with wholesale markets. The wholesaler is buying in order to sell. Let us suppose that we are dealing with an old stabilized market and that we are dealing with an actual dealer, not a speculator. We will assume that the commodity is in an organized market and that we know what the price is.

The rate of consumption, a trend of visible supply, would help to determine price. Interest rates for carrying, the problem of financing, storage charges, liability to deterioration, and the risk element that the buyer may be wrong in his judgment—all of these get significance from the anticipations as to the future trends of things. In the Marshallian analysis, anticipations for the future are abstracted from his writings. Marshall's concept of a demand schedule can be explained only in terms either that dealers expect prices to continue unchanged or on the assumption that if they do not expect the prices to remain the same, they have no idea as to what direction they will move toward.

Operators are very much concerned with anticipations as to the future; the rate at which they buy is not the simple reflex of a consumer's demand schedule. In Marshallian economics, it is necessary to assume that purchases at each price are for consumption at that price. Instead of starting with utility schedules, he would start with an actual price of some particular commodity. The consumer also may anticipate price changes.

June 27, 1930

"Normal" does not refer to an actual expanse of actual time. In such a time, the basic factors will be changing. You are working in a timeless world. There is, therefore, no normal price. Once the normal price is reached, it will continue indefinitely. The normal price under the conditions stated lasts forever, but it takes time for it to be established. The long-run normal price is the one which would be established if you gave the factors time to work themselves out. Marshall's normal price is a useful concept, but it is not really an equilibrium price. The demand adjusts itself so quickly that one does not need to speak of "after a long time." He says that ordinarily a demand which is elastic in the long run will also be elastic in the short run. He takes it for granted that it is not necessary to distinguish between short-run demand and long-run demand. One of his contributions to economics is the different ways in which price adjustments would take place according to the time allowed for adjustment.

A short-run normal price might result in a static world if a disturbance was created from outside which increased the demand and you wanted to see what price would be established after a period in which there was time to vary the output from the existing plants, but no time to expand the plants. Processes of adjustment presumably begin immediately. In the first place, you can press your plant more intensively and then, you can start expanding your plant. We can assume that the long-run normal price would be the price if there were all the time needed for all adjustments to be made. If you actually knew what the normal price was today, you would know what the actual price was going to be two or three years hence.

Another mode of working in economic phenomena is in terms of a balanced aquarium in which no disturbance can occur. There is a rhythm in the world, but it is so perfect that it is impossible to tell which is first and which is last. The factors are mutually dependent. If all items are related to all other items, all are related to each other. Whether you use the word "cause" or not, I do not care. You must say that a certain event will happen upon a certain other event happening.

An increase in demand will necessarily be followed by an increase in price. The average unit of cost may increase in a short-run period. Marshall is assuming that the plant is operating on a comfortable capacity basis. He assumes that the increase comes from a previous position of equilibrium in which the productive powers are already being used to comfortable capacity.

July 1, 1930

For the long run, the most useful definition of normal price is that price which, if it continued for an indefinite period of time, would keep the rate of production and the rate of consumption in balance. There are some critics of this kind of economics who think that they have convicted the "normal" economist. "Normal" here is a technical term having this special meaning, and it is normal only in the sense that if the price happens to be normal, you ought not to expect it to last. Whether it is a right or wrong price is still open to investigation and decision. It has a peculiar relationship to actual price. An analogy is the position of the North Star. The navigator steers by it but does not hope to reach it. In order to know what is going to happen to the prevailing market price, it would be necessary to know what the normal circumstances are at that time, and these circumstances will be different from the year before.

Very little has been done in analysis in the field of market price. Studies in this field must be empirical. What are the circumstances leading to high variability of price?

Types of Price Curves

The kind of market helps to determine the price, whether the market is competitive or monopolistic, etc. There are also questions of regional differences in price. Very little has been done in this connection. What are the price differentials between sight and future exchange rates and what makes the differentials? Geography also has an effect on price. Most price data published are not actual prices. Most price data are some form of an average without itemization as to the amount sold at each price used in the average. The stock ticker is one type of instrument which indicates all transactions.

Supply

There is a tendency among good economists to take too much for granted in this field. The objective of our study is to reach a supply curve. We must build up this curve out of the elements. The following three stages must be taken into consideration:

1. Technological conditions connected with production.
2. Laws or trends of cost. This is in terms of prices per unit.
3. Emergence of a supply curve out of a cost situation.

Marshall labels cost and supply curves S-S'. He shifts too easily from one to the other. The general tendency among economists to confuse cost curves and supply curves is partly due to him. He does not bother to distinguish at all between technological factors, the laws of physical return, and the laws or trends of money costs. Distinguishing between laws of cost and laws of physical return may not be important. For long-run normals, if constant output is assumed to be the optimum degree of intensive use, it is conceivable that you can get along without distinguishing between the laws of physical return and those of financial cost. This is the case if you assume that the factors bear constant prices per unit.

For short-run questions and for the analysis of the operation of physical returns and of costs under varying utilization of a given sized plant, it is vital to distinguish between the laws of return and the financial laws of cost.

Law of Diminishing Returns

Analysis of the German school:

1. A quantity of any complex result is due to a combination of independent but equally necessary factors and ultimately depends on that factor which is available in the smallest proportion relative to the others—the limiting factor.
2. By increasing the supply of any one of these factors except that which is relatively scarcest, you either fail to increase output altogether or to increase it in a much smaller proportion than you have increased the factor.
3. If you increase the smallest factor, you get a greater increase because this increase stimulates the other factors. (Experimentation in this country has tended to disprove this last statement.)
4. When all factors can be proportionately increased, the return can be increased proportionately.
5. In actual practice, the factors remaining beyond the power of increase by human effort are fundamentally responsible for the operation of the law of diminishing return or are fundamentally responsible for the inability of man to evade the consequences of the law of diminishing return.

The limiting factor gets to be a climatic one, to be dealt with by irrigation. Light has been regarded as the limiting factor beyond human control. This is a limiting factor peculiar to agriculture.

Liebig credits J. S. Mill with the first formulation of the law of diminishing returns and questions how he was able to do it without knowing the limiting factor.[5] Turgot may have been the first clear expounder of it.

In connection with the financial laws of cost, a "law" means here a sequence and not a necessary sequence. It would be better to speak of the trends of cost. The trends of unit costs as output changes will depend on the way in which the proportions of the factors are altered or are not altered. The trends of cost will depend (1) on the proportions of the factors; (2) on the size of the working unit; (3) on the size of the industry as a whole; and (4) on the trend price per unit of factor. It is necessary to account for all of these four elements. After your cost curve is obtained, it is necessary to find out what kind of a cost curve it is and how it is possible to get a supply curve from this cost curve.

Increased Aggregate (1) Physical Units:	Average Return (2)	Marginal Return (3)	Value Return	
			Average (4)	Marginal (5)
10 labor + 100 acres = 1,000 bushels	100 bu.			
11 labor + 100 acres = 1,095 bushels	99 ½ bu.	95		
12 labor + 100 acres = 1,185 bushels	98 ¾ bu.	90		
13 labor + 100 acres = 1,265 bushels	97 4/13 bu.	80		

Column (4) would equal Column (2) × the price.

Column (5) would equal Column (3) × the price.

If the above is typical of the industry at large, as the output increases the price would fall, and you would get a decreasing physical amount times a decreasing number of dollars per unit, which would give the diminishing marginal productivity of labor.

Supposing it is desired to know the laws of cost under the above conditions. It is possible to get from these data the average labor cost per unit, assuming the price of the factors remains constant. You could get the marginal cost per bushel, if you knew the wages of labor, from the marginal return per laborer.

It is possible to distinguish between real costs in the sense of factors of production. Coefficients of production are used by the Continental Mathematical economists. The amount of the various factors of production necessary for the production of one unit of commodity would be the coefficient of production. There may be some cost connected with certain types of industry not borne wholly by those in the industry but which are thrown off on others. There may be some compensations to others. The cost to the individual may be greater that the cost to the community. There may be the pain costs of the Classical school in terms of disutility.

Labor increases faster than the aggregate output. The result would be an increase in aggregate output but not in as great a proportion as the application of the variable factor. A decrease of both average and marginal return per unit of the variable factor will take place. There will be an increase in the return per unit of the constant factor. Increased returns to the constant factor is a part of the law. The diminishing returns can go to a point where the aggregate output ceases to increase, and under these circumstances, other things have to be modified. There is diminishing returns to some particular specified factor. Diminishing returns apply here to the labor and capital. To the land, the result is increased returns. The result should be stated in general terms, in terms of diminishing returns to some one factor.

The law of diminishing returns does not give directly a law of cost but gives the real cost per unit of the output of the increased factor.

The law of diminishing returns has no general resemblance to the engineering term of efficiency. One does not get a best combination out of the technological factors alone. The economist needs financial accounting to find out efficiency. When an engineer speaks of efficiency, he means, for instance, the number of units of heat to be gotten out of a ton of coal. He does not need to know financial propositions. Engineers have learned that their efficiency concepts are lopsided concepts, and they are now studying financial engineering, in which they need an elementary notion of the cost function. It is impossible to devise an efficiency formula which can take into account two different kinds of results. The factors must be homogeneous. Neither in engineering nor in economics is it possible to get an efficiency formula. The law of diminishing returns does not tell you where to stop. The other factors may tell you to go on beyond a certain point.

The first case that we will study will be a given concern, one plant. They are varying the output from this plant, and there is no question as to changing the size of the plant. The question is of getting different units of material by using different amounts of material and labor. This concern is unimportant in the industry, and the industry is unimportant in society. No matter what the concern does, it will be able to buy any number of factors at a constant price. A change in the scale of operations will not affect the price of the factors in the market. Whatever variations in its output, the result would be insufficient to modify appreciably the price of its product.

July 2, 1930

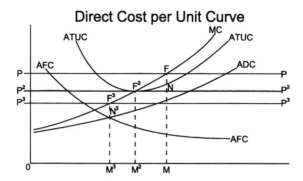

Direct Cost per Unit Curve

To the above curve it is necessary to add overhead. It is negatively inclined.

There can be no percentage of fixed expenses over a period of time. Such a proposition is absurd. At any other rate of operation, the proportions would necessarily be different. Fixed expenses are fixed in aggregate amount. Per unit they are more variable than the variable expenses.

A rectangular hyperbola slopes very much at the start. As you increase output, the reduction in fixed cost per unit gets to be negligible. Economies resulting from spreading the overhead get to be unimportant as your plant is already being used to something approaching comfortable capacity. The total unit costs will be the total expenses involved. The more important are the fixed costs, the longer the total cost curve will have a negative inclination. If most costs are variable, costs will not go on if production ceases, and the fixed costs may play only a negligible part and a negative inclination may appear only for the early stages.

Most economists would draw the average direct cost curve as having a slightly negative inclination at the start. This is of doubtful validity, however. This so far is a general picture of cost conditions as you vary output from a given plant. All of these are average cost curves. The marginal cost curve is secured by cumulating the total cost curve. The greater the output, the larger will be the aggregate cost. Where the marginal cost curve intersects the average total unit cost curve, they must be equal. For a constant cost curve, the average cost and the marginal cost are the same. At the point where a horizontal line can be drawn tangent to the curve, you know that the average cost equals the marginal cost. The marginal cost curve must intersect at this point.

$$MC = \frac{d(av.\ cost \times qu.)}{d\ qu.} = av.\ cost + \left(cu. \times \frac{d\ av.\ cost}{d\ qu.}\right)$$

$$MC = qu. \times \frac{d\ av.\ cost}{d\ qu.} = 0$$

At the lowest point,

$$MC = av.\ cost$$

It is possible to draw the marginal cost curve from the direct cost curve. Arguing on the assumption of rational behavior, this can be done. If the fixed costs are really fixed, they are sunk costs. If the amount per unit does not change, they are sunk costs, and, therefore, they ought to have no part in influencing behavior.

The aggregate direct costs equal the unit direct cost times the number of units. The aggregate total costs equal the unit direct costs times the quantity plus the unit fixed costs times the quantity. The positive cost curve will have a positive inclination for all industries where the situation is one of variation of output from a given plant.

In the above diagram, suppose P-P to be the prevailing price. At this price, it pays the producer to produce OM. MN is cost, and everything above N (NF) is clear profit. At this price, the producer will put in more capital, and the price will come down. For a typical producer or for producers on the average, the price curve is cutting the marginal cost curve at F^2.

The price would change to P^2-P^2. P-P is inconsistent with long-run equilibrium. Either the cost must rise or the price must fall. If the price is P^3-P^3, the producer loses F^3-N^3. All of these are short-run equilibrium prices.

There is no discussion in Marshall of spreading the overhead, because in the short run he already starts with a plant working at comfortable capacity. Any change will be an increase in this rather than a decrease. In the long run, the plant is being used to the optimum point. You have the optimum scale for your output. Under those circumstances, no element of varying the output from the same plant enters into the discussion. If you are changing the output, you are also changing the plant facilities.

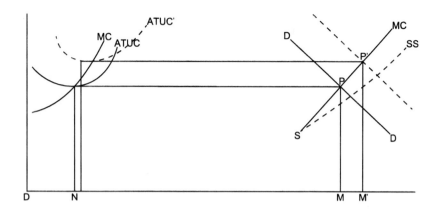

Let us suppose that under conditions of a positive cost curve, the marginal cost curve will be the important one in determining supply. The price shall be equal to the marginal cost and the lowest point on the average total unit cost curve. If the price is not at this point, either more firms will enter the industry or some will be forced out. The price must be equal to the marginal cost and the lowest average cost. Now the plant is in equilibrium with the industry, and the actual price is MP. Now, it is of no special use for the producer to expand. If all firms are in this position, there would be no inducement for new firms to come in or for old firms to go out.

Suppose that the demand curve goes up for the market and in the short run, it results in the increase in the market price to $P'M'$. The producer should then expand his output (as shown in the above diagram). If the price rises, the marginal cost is increased. The producer has an extra profit on his total operations because of his earlier units. This will not last if other companies can come in, and this will probably occur. The profit will be temporary and will disappear as soon as the new concerns come in.

Supposing that it is a question of farming where it is impossible to multiply the concerns and all the land of a given quality has already been used, then the new $ATUC'$ curve will become the new equilibrium situation. Expansion will be as permanent as the increase in demand. The marginal cost curve will remain the same but under this situation, the fixed factors will have a different price. Land will go up, the price of this fixed factor will be higher, and the average total unit cost curve and the marginal cost curve will still cut it at its lowest point. This is for the case where the product is produced by a given amount of some factors and cannot be increased, where you can expand output by more intensive cultivation of the best land or by moving to the inferior land. Following the principle that from time to time the results shall be distributed in such a way that for each unit of investment there is the same unit of return, you will get some increase by working old acres more intensively and some by moving to new acres. The last increment of return will be the same to whichever use it is put. The industry's marginal cost curve will run somewhat lower. It is a positive long-run question for agriculture.

On the assumption that there are a million acres of quality A and another million of quality B, and if you increase the output it pays you to go on to the B land as well as working the A land more intensively, the rent on the A land is less than it otherwise would be and the price is less. If others can come in, if any producer can produce ON output at MP price, what goes above is of no interest. If the demand under these circumstances rises, Smith will produce another ON instead of Jones producing more than ON. The cost curve for the industry will then be a horizontal line. A technological horizontal cost is conceivable under these circumstances where it is possible to indefinitely multiply the new concerns.

We started out with what I claim to be a cost situation generally applicable to individual concerns, on the assumption that they are varying output from the same plant. For the individual concern, the marginal cost, average cost, and the price are all equal. This is the only place where a long-run equilibrium can last. For a short-run equilibrium, the average cost does not need to equal price, but price must always equal marginal cost.

Let us study the situation from the point of view of a whole industry and assume that the output can take place only by more intensive working of the plant and plants cannot be increased. Under these circumstances, the long-run marginal cost curve gets to be the long-run supply curve. The marginal cost for the short run will be the same as the long run if you can expand the number of the productive units. There is no such case as this, however. So far, I have indicated the long-run cost conditions determining supply for one type of production.

The industry marginal cost curve is the sum of all the individual marginal cost curves. Equilibrium in the long-run must be such that the supply curve shall be the industry's marginal cost curve such that at the margin, the marginal cost shall equal the price. After an equilibrium position has been reached, the average cost would be equal to the price. This would be done through a revaluation of the land.

There are no changes in the prices of the factors in an increasing cost industry producing from a fixed plant. *MP* is the actual price and here, equilibrium has been reached. The average cost curve would then move up. Land would have increased in value per acre to the producer, and a revaluation of the productive units would bring up the average cost until it was equal to the marginal cost and the price. The average costs would adjust themselves to the situation.

I want to go back to an individual concern. This concern is able to expand its plant. There are internal technological economies of large-scale production. I want to draw a graph showing the change in the cost situation as the output in that plant is increased.

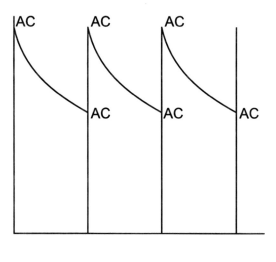

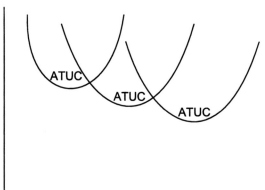

July 8, 1930

Cost Curve with Internal Economies of Large-Scale Production for a Single Plant

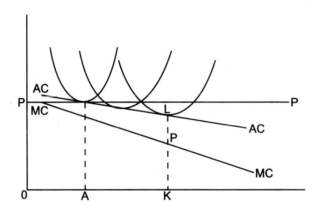

The long-run cost curve would presumably also be the long-run supply curve. In the long run, you always assume that you are producing each output with the optimum scale of that output. The lowest average costs at which that output could be produced from each of these successive scales would be the optimum scale. We can assume continuity. There is an infinite number of U-shaped curves which can be drawn. A line drawn through the optimum costs at which each possible output could be produced would give the average cost curve, but it is the average cost at which that output could be produced from a plant at the optimum scale for that output. The marginal cost curve would run below and would not be the curve that the individual entrepreneur should follow. The average cost is KL. The marginal cost is only KP. When there is a negative cost curve of this sort, the marginal cost is not the thing that determines the entrepreneur's behavior.

The average cost determines the supply curve. L represents the amount of the minimum scale on which the producer would be willing to operate if the price were KL. Assuming that his output is a negligible part of the total and assuming that this is the price line, P, the prevailing price, there is no reason why he should stop at any point below this line in building up his plant. The price is higher than KL; why should he not expand his output? All producers will find themselves in this position. Eventually, the industry will be in the hands of a single concern. The industry curve is inconsistent with competition of this type. It is possible to expand by working the plant more intensively or by putting up a new plant. *MC* is the marginal cost from the expansion of the plant, or, in other words, by putting up more plants.

So far, we have had the cost trends as output is varied from a given plant with no changes in the prices of the factors. The situation is of the output varied for a given concern both by varying the output from a given plant and by enlarging the plant on the assumption that there are economies of large-scale production showing themselves at the lowest point in successive plant curves, each being lower than the preceding one.

Let us take an individual concern, a fixed plant, but with the additional assumption that the conditions of what have been called "external economies" are present. A change in the size of the industry as a whole modifies the cost for this concern, and there are external economies of large-scale production. We shall attempt to represent what would happen if in that industry there were external economies of large production and if the size of the industry increased, if a lot of other companies came in. This is a long-run adjustment.

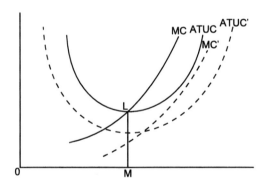

L is the lowest point. The industry expands, and cost should fall to the dotted line in the above diagram. The downfall in the cost is represented, because the industry has expanded its output. This is still the individual concern. It still is necessary for equilibrium that production shall be at the lowest average cost. If there is any reduction in the unit costs of labor and materials, the new marginal cost curve must be below the old curve.

The producers may be able to buy certain kinds of tools, which, if enough were produced, could be produced cheaper. They would then be getting internal economies of large-scale production. Internal economies of large-scale production are external economies of large production to the industries using those tools. The economy is a saving in price. These three cases are used to represent the individual concern in a likely situation. All are likely types of situations for individual concerns.

If there are net diseconomies of scale, the scale will not be increased; the increase will be by the multiplying of plants rather than by an increase in the size of a plant.

The next curve to be presented has a bearing on Pigou's doctrines in his *Economics of Welfare*, particularly in connection with his argument that there is no such thing as a technologically increasing cost industry on the grounds that industries do not expand if their costs rise.[6] There is no reason for an industry to incur the net diseconomies of large production.

When the output of the industry is *OA*, the price would have to be *AH*, in the diagram below.

Jones & Co.

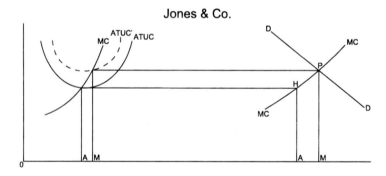

Suppose that the actual output for the industry is *OM*. If the price is *MP*, the marginal cost would equal the price for Jones. *MC* is also the marginal cost of the output of the industry as a whole. There may be in the range of infinitesimals some difference in the increments whether Jones or Smith adds the last increment, but this is not important for our study.

Now, there is an output at a point at which the average cost is higher than the lowest cost. This is not a long-run equilibrium situation. Now production is at a cost other than the lowest average cost. Pigou says that an individual concern will not expand its output if this means increasing cost, but that the expansion of the industry will come from multiplying concerns.

Let us assume a country that is fairly definitely specialized in one crop. All good land is in tillage. We will abstract from the existence of the inferior land to which cultivation could be extended. Hawaiian sugar land is a good example. All land is being worked. Suppose the demand for sugar goes up and each producer finds it possible to move up on the marginal cost curve until it equals price. Now he is not operating at the lowest marginal cost. There is no land that anybody else can use. The *ATUC* curve will move up by the rent being raised and the cost of land per acre being raised. The marginal cost curve and the prices of the variable factors do not change. Only the price of the fixed factor, land, changes. Here, all the important conditions of equilibrium are met. The assumptions are that the prices of the factors do not change except in respect to that factor which is kept absolutely fixed; that the industry is one in which there is a limited amount of one of the factors; that it is impossible to reproduce the original farms; and that it is impossible to go on to poorer land, because there is no poorer land. An increased output under these circumstances can take place only by moving up the marginal cost curve and the *ATUC* curve. There is no possibility of external economies, because the number of concerns cannot be multiplied.

Let us assume that it is possible to move on to inferior land. The farmer does not have to indefinitely intensify production on his best acres. He can move on to inferior land. The average cost curve will rise less steeply under these conditions. The availability of the poorer land keeps the cost and therefore the price from rising as sharply as it otherwise would in the face of an increasing demand.

Thompson says that the existence of poorer land cannot make good land pay rent.[7] The existence of poorer land reduces the rent that good land can pay. Thompson is right. If any number of farms could be started, there would be a constant cost.

We have now had three individual concern curves. The next two will be external economies of large production and external diseconomies.

Negative Cost Curve and Negative Supply Curve with Stable Equilibrium

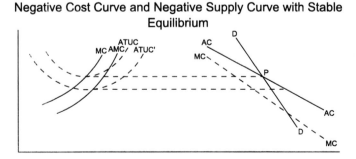

The industry cost curve would determine the industry supply curve where there are external economies, no internal economies, and where the one outstanding factor with respect to trends of cost is the factor of external economies. There is no equilibrium unless the marginal cost equals the price. In this diagram, the marginal cost, the average cost, and the price are equal.

Assuming that the output of the industry increases, as a result, the cost to this concern of producing the given number of units is less than it was before. *E* will equal the new point of long-run equilibrium and will represent the new equilibrium point. (The two situations, although represented on the same chart, cannot simultaneously occur.) *AC* would be the average for the industry but marginal also for each individual concern. *MC'* would be the marginal cost curve for the industry. *MC'* is not of significance in guiding economic behavior, and the average cost curve is the significant curve.

External technological economics are assumed, adhering to the assumption that prices of the factors remain the same. The practical importance of this situation is on the pecuniary side; that pecuniary costs fall where there are external economies.

I am not sure that I can think of external diseconomies on a technological basis. On a pecuniary basis, it is a very obvious type of case. This is just a reverse of the previous diagram.

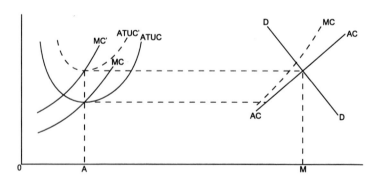

If the size of the industry increases, the cost rises for each individual concern even though the output remains the same. In this diagram, the output is reduced a little, but there is no stress to be put on this fact. *AC* again is average to the industry and marginal to the individual concerns. (Both external economies and external diseconomies have significance in the contribution of Pigou's system.)

There are external economies and diseconomies, respectively, which the business man does not get. In actual situations, you will find combinations of the above types of cost situations. The net result is the important thing and everything should be stated in terms of net.

For marginal cost only, H is the point of lowest short-run cost; if both the ATUC and MC curves are considered, it is also the point of lowest long-run cost. In the long run, the equilibrium scale is the one at which it is possible to produce at the lowest average cost. In the short run, you can bring yourself into equilibrium by bringing the marginal cost to the point where it equals the price. Under internal economies, it is always in the producer's interest to expand his scale, while under external economies it is in his disinterest to expand his scale.

If you define "short run" as Marshall does, in which there is no time to change the plant facilities, under internal economies, equilibrium is still possible. Internal economies come from an increase of scale, meaning an expansion of plant. The equilibrium notion is a tool of economic analysis; it is not an end. Its chief purpose is to give us an indication as to the direction in which forces and phenomena will move in the actual world under given circumstances.

Stable equilibrium, internal economies of large-scale production, and competitive conditions cannot exist together. But, in actual fact, we do not have a stable equilibrium any way, and we do not have static conditions. In connection with internal economies, there is a process of elimination of the smaller producers by the larger ones, of the growing acquisition of control of output by the few largest concerns,. They are moving toward a situation in which they are involved in cut-throat competition. There is a tendency toward monopoly in such an industry. The tendency may not ever be achieved because new conditions come up each year. The situation of internal economies is important even for competition and its significance is the downward trend of the average cost curve and increased demand that are likely to lead to a lowering of the price. This is true only in the long run.

July 10, 1930

Assuming that producers act rationally, the fact that a thing costs $10.00 should have no influence on its price except that it will influence what it will cost to produce another one like it. The experience you have will affect your judgment as to future costs. Fixed costs connected with a plant which already has been established should have no influence on the activities of the entrepreneur.

From these cost and supply curve diagrams, the short-run supply is determined by the individual and the industry marginal costs. The marginal cost curve is positive, and any point on the curve represents the maximum output which the individual or industry is prepared to turn out at that price. The marginal-cost positive curve and maximum output are most important in the short run both for the individual and for the industry.

In the long run, there are four main classes of cases which might exist, of which three are consistent with stable equilibrium.

1. A part of the plant is fixed or relatively fixed, even in the long run. The land is suitable for only one crop, and the good acres are strictly limited. Here, the individual and the industry marginal cost curve would be just like the short-run curve. There would be no distinction between the short-run and long-run adjustment. If it is possible to move on to new, but inferior, acres, the slope would be less steep upward.

2. External economies. The significant cost curves are the individual marginal cost curve and the industry average cost curve. The supply curve would be negative for the industry, and the points would be interpreted as minimum output points. The marginal cost to the industry is less than the marginal cost to the individual under external economies, but this has no bearing on behavior.

3. External diseconomies. The individual marginal cost is the significant individual cost curve and the industry average cost is the significant industry curve. It is a positive supply curve with maximum output. The individual producer is not interested in the industry marginal cost and this is not significant. The cost he has to bear is less than the industry as a whole has to bear.

4. Internal economies. The individual average cost, not the marginal cost, is significant, because if the individual operated on the basis of his marginal cost, his marginal cost would be lower than his average cost. The individual would

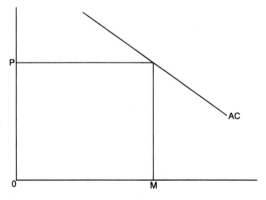

OM is the minimum scale at which the producer will be willing to produce with a price of OP.

operate on his average cost. The industry would also operate on an average cost basis. The curve would represent the minimum output. A negative supply curve, with unstable equilibrium, is always an inducement to every individual to keep on expanding output.

With a historical price-quantity series, how is it possible to get a supply curve out of such data? Where there is a production period, where there is a significant period between committing yourself to the output and having it available for sale, if production is for stock, it is necessary to look for a lag in taking historical data and trying to get out of them a supply curve. It is necessary to look for a lag between the price and output data. The price which should be taken in the case of corn is that of the planting period, and the quantity to be taken is that of the harvest period. In order to get a supply curve, it would be necessary to take this lag into account. The price of 1930 and the output of 1930 would be the associated pair of data.

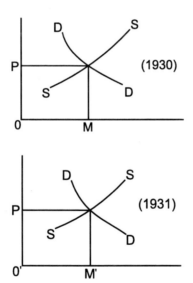

If the facts were like this, you could not get a demand curve or supply curve unless you know the shift. On the basis of known facts and known techniques, you are gambling on the most probable situation, and its probability may be very low. The problem of the statistical measurement of supply curves is still in a more primitive condition than that of the measurement of demand curves. The supply curve of agriculture is the response of output to changes in price just as the demand curve is the response of consumption to changes in price. In agriculture, there is trouble with the weather. The response of a plant to a change of price might be more important than the response of output to a change in price. A crop failure may bring about a decrease in supply when the price rises.

5. External economies. It has been said that external economies in one business unit are necessarily internal economies in some other unit. Where there is a continuous tendency toward economies from scale, eventually there will be a monopoly.

Let us discuss the manufacture of plows. A larger plow industry may mean that machines for making plows will become cheaper. An external economy to the plow-making industry may be an internal economy to the plow-making machine industry. The plow-making machine industry may get monopolized, and a further expansion of output may give further economies for the plow industry. If a monopoly has a negative cost curve, it pays the monopoly to charge a lower price for larger orders. There would still be external economies to the plow-making industry, even though they are the product of internal economies to the industry serving it and this industry has gotten monopolized.

What is an example of an external economy to A that is not an internal economy to B? If there is a country in which unskilled labor comes in large amounts and is to choose its occupation, it will be attracted to the large industry that is somewhat out of proportion to the size of the large industry. There is another labor gain for a large industry and that is the size of the labor pool, the ability to get labor quickly. Other advantages are the cross-fertilization of ideas and processes. The more producers there are, the more likely it is that new ways of doing things are going to be discovered. There is the possibility of economies of buying and selling. There are economies in having the industry organized about one center or one place. There is the possibility of having a trade journal, trade paper, or trade association. These probably are not of very great importance, and most external economies to A would upon examination be found to be internal economies to B. Such internal economies are bargaining power, buying power, and the division of labor. Edgeworth, in the *Economic Journal* for December 1911, lists integration, but this is not a phase of large-scale production.[8] Integration is the introduction of many types of products in the same plant. Large-scale production means that you are under the same organization, and a great many units of the same type of process are going on. Integration is the multiplication of the types of processes.

Edgeworth suggests the stimulus of companionship. However, all these economies are exhausted before you reach the stage of the large-scale plant. There is the advantage of interchangeable parts and of self-insurance. Risks must be scattered geographically, but self-insurance would be effective. A large concern can probably get better credit terms. Size makes it seem a better risk. A large-scale concern can make use of national advertising media. The prestige of size may be an economy in selling. It may bring customers and may enable the plant to get a higher price.

July 11, 1930

There is a possible conflict between the English and Austrian approaches to the value problem. The Austrians introduced utility analysis. Walras and Jevons both preceded the Austrians in utility analysis.[9] In England, there was some utility analysis back in the 1830's. It is not on the issue of utility analysis that I am looking for differences. The Austrian school started out by denying something that the English school had brought out. The Austrians argue that the ultimate source of value lies in utilities and in demand schedules on the demand side. The cost of production is itself a reflection of demand. Value is conducted from the product to the intermediate commodities instead of the other way, in which the English school measures it. The Austrians say that the price of the product determines the price of the factor, which is another expression for cost.

The English made it a dualistic system consisting of demand variables and supply variables. They took demand for granted but analyzed supply more thoroughly. The Austrians say that the cost changes as the price and because of the price. Both schools accept the proposition that $\frac{P^1}{P^2} = \frac{Money\ cost^1}{Money\ cost^2}$. The prices of two commodities will be to each other as their relative costs of production. The Austrians go further and ask what determines what the money costs of production are. They say that the rate per unit, its price, will be its value creating power in the least of its best uses. It is the money value of the unit of a factor in the least good of the best available uses for that factor. The value of a factor is equal to the value in its marginal use. It is the peculiar Austrian doctrine that the value of the factors of production is determined only by their value in the least of the best available uses. The word "only" is the point at issue. The English would accept the proposition that a factor gets its value in part from its value to the person who uses it and, there being many uses, the value of the factor will be the value in its marginal use. The Austrians say, however, that this is the only source of value.

The English would have replied: "But what shall be the least good of the best available uses for the factor?" This is a question to be solved. It depends on how many units of the factor there are, and the number of units depends on the rate of remuneration. The supply curve of the factor is the thing that the Austrians left out and which the English stress as the most important for the long run. The Austrians take as given what the marginal use of a factor shall be, while the English say that this is one of the unknowns in the situation. The Austrians say that ultimately, utility is the single determinant of value and of price. Theirs is a monistic theory and it tries to find the explanation of value in a single element in contradistinction to the dualistic system.

Ricardo stresses that a factor gets distributed to its most important uses. Ricardo, with regard to the above, would have said: "What determines that there shall be, for instance, 100 laborers? Why not 80 or 150?" One of the things determining how many laborers there shall be is the rate of remuneration offered for the labor. It has been difficult for the Austrian school to see what the answer was that the English school was making to them. Fetter[10] is the outstanding exponent of the Austrian school in this country. Davenport is to be included under this heading.

July 14, 1930

I think that the Austrians and the English would have found that there was no issue between them providing they could agree as to the assumptions to start with. The English have held that the assumption as to what the wage rate is will make a difference in the amount of labor available for any use. The Austrians start out with a tacit assumption that there is a given number of laborers and a given amount of capital and land and that these are to be apportioned, if men act rationally, in such a way that they will be applied to their most valuable uses. Granting the Austrian assumptions, I see nothing wrong with the Austrian theory of value. It becomes the English theory of value where the factors of production are all available in given amounts.

Wicksteed and Davenport claim that a supply curve is not needed.[11] They claim that a supply curve is merely a demand schedule broken up into two parts. They include in the whole discussion two classes of existence of the object: (a) units that buyers do not have but would take at certain named prices, and (b) units that potential sellers have and would surrender at particular prices. There are also units that the producers might bring in and reproduce, units which do not exist but would be brought in if the demand existed for them at a satisfactory price. If you are taking into account the possibility of bringing new units into existence, then obviously, you are dealing with stock whose proportions depend on the price. The English have taken the last class as the one requiring the most emphasis. They have acquired the habit of discussing supply as the most significant in terms of what scale of output will result from a given price.

The critics of the Austrian school began to point out to them that they were discussing fixed supplies, but it was fifteen years before they began to realize that they had left out the case which the English school had stressed. The question is as to the more preferable assumption. Böhm-Bawerk said that price was the function of one variable. That variable is demand, and by "demand" we mean "utility." The Austrians argue that if price must be as marginal utility, it certainly could not always be as cost of production.

MacVane and Laughlin, and Nicholson in England, resisted the introduction of the utility sort of analysis.[12] English economics accepted the Austrian concept and incorporated it in their own economics. The Austrians kept on fighting the cost of production and supply theories of value, but finally made concessions.

In March 1892, Wieser said that it was not necessary to take into consideration the arduousness of the labor to explain its value.[13] Böhm-Bawerk claimed that the amount of labor consisted of the population, and distinguished between the expenses of production and pain costs. He accepted pain costs as a determinant. He claimed that the expenses of production were merely a reflection of the value.

No English economist could separate himself from the pain cost theory. Wieser has argued that relative disutilities might affect prices, but, nevertheless, the money costs of production, expenses of production, were purely a reflection of demand schedules and they get their amounts and levels wholly from the demand side. The Austrians are wrong at this point. The money costs of production of products using labor will rise. The expenses of production themselves are already reflecting influences from both directions. How many units of labor will be used depends on the demand schedule for the product of labor. That the actual price of labor per unit will be depends on the intersection of the demand and supply curves for labor. On the cost side, there is the intersection between the demand factors and supply factors. From the point of view of theoretical analysis, the English school got the best of it. They were right to start with and with a very few exceptions, they did not get confused. They stated that the Austrian analysis was an improvement of their demand analysis. The Austrians were more acute than the English in their analysis of the ways in which the demand curves for the factors were derived from the demand curves for the products.

On the fundamental thing on which the two were at issue, the English had the better of the argument. The English took over some of the Austrian's theories, which I think gave the English a sound theory. It is now sometimes argued that the Austrians were right and the English were wrong, because at any one time there is a definite amount of labor available, regardless of the rate of wages. The wage rate of a kind of labor will be determined by the amount available and by the various uses for it. We do not know what the supply curves of labor and capital are like. If you start out with the assumption that the supply curves are vertical lines, you are an adherent of the Austrian school. It does not matter for the English type whether the supply schedules are positively or negatively inclined.

The Austrian theory ties up with the opportunity cost doctrine, and this is one type of formulation of the Austrian theory. The opportunity cost theorist states that the cost of production of one product is the value of some other product that could have been produced with the same amount of factors. The price of any factor used in the production of iron, for instance, is its value for the production of wheat, or its value in its best alternative use. With regard to the question of whether or not a manufacturer should count his own labor as a cost, the opportunity cost doctrine gives the proper answer, that he should count the cost at the value they would be worth in disposing of them.

Opportunity cost is not enough as a theory of value, however. It is not sufficient unless you accept the Austrian theories as substantial facts. If it is taken for granted that there are given amounts of the fundamental factors which are not affected by the rates of remuneration, the theory is satisfactory.

In Adam Smith's beaver and deer case, the cost of a deer is the number of beaver that could have been caught in the same time. The relative costs of deer and beaver will be reciprocals of the relative amounts that could be caught in the same length of time. Here, however, the opportunity cost doctrine uses circular reasoning. Suppose it is necessary to catch a beaver by grading through beaver streams and working under unpleasant conditions, while hunting deer may be very exciting. It might be possible to catch three beaver in the time it takes to catch one deer, and yet one deer might exchange for a one-and-a-half beaver. Böhm-Bawerk attributes about 5 percent of the value to disutility. Economic theorists tend too quickly to assume propositions that we have never investigated in detail under guarded conditions.

July 15, 1930

We shall now study cost in relationship to supply from another angle, from the angle with which Marshall is trying to deal in his concept of a representative firm. Marshall was trying to deal with the problem of different costs as between different producers at the same time and was trying to escape from that problem in a legitimate way. He wanted to find some rule as to the variability of cost as between different concerns. He wanted to find some representative concern or representative cost which may be taken as indicative of the trends in the industry as a whole.

Each producer for the short run or long run had to make his marginal cost equal price. He will revalue his sunk costs in such a way as to make them a capitalization of their present return power. The principles of conservative accounting are hostile to writing-up, but this, nevertheless, takes place quite often under the pressure of business conditions.

If an increase in price occurs, land will go up in value. If the farmer is a tenant, he will have to pay a higher rent for the land. If the farmer is an owner, he will have to charge to rent a larger amount per unit of output than he did before. Most of economic theory in the past has been based on the assumption of original cost. Business men do operate on the basis of costs that are not necessarily original costs; they may be reproduction costs, bookkeeping costs, or opportunity costs.

All producers tend to make their marginal costs equal price. Without this proposition, there is no rhyme nor reason in our cost analysis. The pattern will be one of a tendency to conformity of the marginal cost to price. At any one time, the average costs would differ in the short run. Short-run equilibrium excludes the possibility of varying the scale.

Marshall was interested in marginal cost curves in spite of his admission that they tend toward monopoly in the long run. Marshall worked mainly with internal cost curves and with negative cost and negative supply curves resulting from internal economies. On the basis of average and original costs, Marshall had the problem of dealing with average costs that can be different for different producers, of describing the industry as a whole by some convenient formula or graph. This is the problem of index numbers. The average concept is necessarily an empirical concept. Marshall would not use an average because it involved measurement; therefore, he used the representative firm. Marshall wanted to find a modal concern, a concern which was like many other firms. Marshall was very vague, and at the present time it is one of the great games in England to point out flaws in Marshall's representative firm concept. He did not succeed in what he was trying to do.

We may start with any concern on the assumption that the relative positions of all concerns remain similar to each other under all conditions. On this assumption it does not matter what concern is taken. It is a credit to Marshall that he saw the problem, but I do not think that he did very much with it. He did some injury because a generation of readers has thought that there was a solution in his concept. The position of one concern does not remain the same in relation to the industry as the industry grows or contracts. If you follow any particular concern, it would not be actually representative of the industry as a whole. Marshall thought that it would be possible to take the firm which is representative of a certain year and compare it with a firm that is representative of the next year. Here it is necessary to have precise specifications for the location of the firm, and he does not give these specifications.

Pigou would assume that the industry was in equilibrium and that it would be possible to find a concern which is in a position to continue indefinitely on its own level as long as the industry remains on that level. There is no inducement for the firm to expand or contract. If the firm and industry are in equilibrium, you know that the elements of equilibrium, $ABCD$, must be offset by the disequilibrium elements, $EFGH$. Follow the fortunes of the equilibrium firm, and you will follow the fortunes of the equilibrium industry. This is simply an average concept. Pigou has created a firm, all of whose operations are the average for the industry at large.

Marginal cost shall equal price; the average cost, to the extent that its original cost may be above or below the price, but insofar as it is a revaluated price in terms of earning power, average costs shall equal price for all producers in the long run. Marshall was probably somewhat concerned with the actual as well as with the theoretical price. The result was that he had a mixture of both actual and theoretical price. Marshall says that negative and positive cost curves are nonreversible, but this is not the case.

July 16, 1930

Taussig, during the course of his work during the war, arranged a series of plants in ascending order, as in the following diagram, and found an ordinary supply curve.[14] The results have led to a new version of the representative firm theory called the "bulk line theory." It was found that the bulk of the output was produced at a price equal to or less than the prevailing price, but that some portion of the output was being produced at a cost in excess of price. This resulted in a modification of the marginal cost theory. If it is argued that marginal cost determines price and if it is found that marginal costs are in excess of price, it is necessary to either abandon the theory or to give a different meaning to "marginal." The old marginal utility economist had a theory which was rational in the absence of conflicting facts. Taussig found that in any situation, some output is being produced at a cost in excess of price. "Marginal" now means the bulk line cost. This cost is the cost at which the bulk of the output is produced. In practice, the bulk line is located by making it equal to the price.

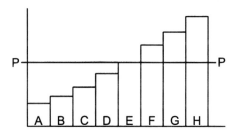

In this diagram, Firm *E* would be the determinant of the market price, because cost is the same as price. They could not tell what the bulk line is without knowing the price. Rarely would a situation be found in which the price was as high as the highest cost. The bulk line theorists found a cost equal to price, which is no theory at all. If you can find a bulk line concern that can be located independently of the actually prevailing price, you are back with a representative firm. Marshall says that the representative firm is one that is not particularly prosperous and yet does not operate at a loss. The bulk line firm, on that basis, is substantially Marshall's representative firm. The bulk line theory apparently did show that the marginal cost did not determine the price; it did not show the relationship of price to cost.

Secrist has been endeavoring to find a representative firm that holds its place from year to year.[15] Simpson finds that the bulk line is at 88.7 percent. The bulk line is substantially different from industry to industry and moves with the cycle quite definitely. In a boom year, it is conceivable that all the output will be at a cost that is lower than price. The percentage of costs covered rises with an upward swing of the cycle. It will be found that from 3 percent to 20 percent of output is being produced at a cost in excess of price.

This situation is not inconsistent with the theory of marginal utility. Marginal cost theory is a theory as to what would happen if forces were given time to work themselves out. Actual statistical investigation brings out circumstances at the moment of statistical investigation. In the previous diagram, H is the highest cost at which anything is produced. Marginal cost is to be defined as the increment of cost resulting from the addition of one to the aggregate output. Marginal cost may be lower than average cost. The situation is quite consistent with the doctrine of marginal cost equaling price in the short run. It is not consistent with a long-run adjustment. If marginal cost equals price, it is still possible to have receiverships and bankruptcies if interest on bonded indebtedness or on investment is included. The theory tries to explain that there is no providential arrangement whereby cost equals price if men should make a misjudgment. There is a possibility of a discrepancy between cost and price through incorrect anticipations or incorrect accounting.

One ought never to say that marginal cost determines price or that the marginal producer determines price. Böhm-Bawerk has two sets of marginal pairs determining price. The units have to be homogeneous.

Marginal labor is as competent as any other labor. The marginal increment ought to be thought of in terms of the difference in aggregate quantity x times Δx. Individual H with the highest cost has no particular significance for price theory. H is worth watching when there is a declining price without declining cost; otherwise, it has no special significance. If H keeps on as it is, it will be forced out. H, however, may be in a temporary situation and may change its position. B may be having good luck this year, whereas next year it may be forced out. There tends to be a permanence to the extra bulk-line situation. There are individuals who will be in that area year after year. The population will change, but there will always be a population except in boom years. It can be assumed that for no person shall price equal cost; yet, for the industry at large, price shall always equal average cost. I see no reason to expect much stability. The bulk line will be somewhere between 80 percent and 95 percent, but that is a wide range and it will change with the business cycle.

The only reason why there is a relationship between cost and price is because there is a relationship between cost and supply. The relationship between cost and price is not direct. Cost accounting textbooks tell you how to find the correct costs, but they do not tell what to do with the costs. Cost accounting theory until within the last two or three years has been written in terms of average cost, whereas the firm should determine price on the basis of marginal cost.

July 17, 1930

Monopoly

The supply curve for blades in the following diagram will be a horizontal line. Considering a demand for commodity *a* entering into manufacture with another commodity, *b*, the demand for *a* will increase if the supply price of *b* falls.

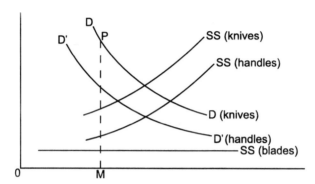

In the case of joint costs, Marshall assumes that everything is known and that the derived supply schedule for the product is the thing to be ascertained. The problem is to find a derived supply curve for meat when the demand curve for cows and the supply curve for hides are known. The demand curve for meat is known. On the assumption that the cost of production determines supply, it is desired to find the supply curve for meat through a process of apportionment of costs. Meat and hides are raised together as joint products. What can be obtained for a hide is subtracted from the cost of production of a cow, and that is the cost of the meat. This is the derived supply curve for meat. It is essentially the accountant's way of apportioning joint costs.

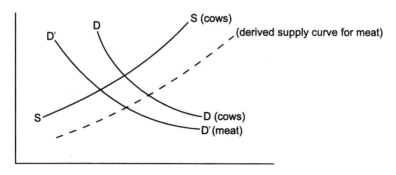

The problem is to find the derived supply curve for meat, having a supply curve for cows. To do this, the demand curve for hides should be subtracted from the supply curve for cows.

Marshall says that the difficulty in apportioning costs exists only when the proportions of the factors are fixed technologically. If the proportions of hides to meat are fixed, they must be the same, and a problem of apportioning cost is difficult. It is not only difficult, it is impossible. If the proportions are variable, the task of seeking separate costs is an absurdity. The whole cost accounting procedure when practiced on the assumption that the proportions of the factors are fixed is absurd and cannot answer any rational purpose. If meats and hides must be produced in the same proportions, the only question to be answered is that of the number of cows which shall be produced. In the case of cattle, you can change the quality of the meat or the hide by arbitrarily changing the feeding process. In the case of wool and mutton as joint products, it is impossible to get both wool and mutton simultaneously; whereas it is possible to get both hide and beef simultaneously. Marshall's solution of the case, where by feeding cattle differently the amount of meat to be gotten is changed, is a simple solution if his statement of the case is accepted. He converts it to a marginal cost proposition.

Suppose that at the equilibrium point x oxen are sold at price y. Then, $y = \emptyset(x')$. Each ox yields m units of beef. Then, $m = \Delta y'$. The rate increase of cost in feeding will increase the amount of beef by a small amount, leaving the hide constant. $\frac{\Delta y'}{\Delta m} =$ marginal cost (or supply price) of beef. It may be found that by increasing the cost per cow per year by 50¢ per lb., more of beef is obtained. The marginal cost is thus 50¢ per lb. It is desired to know what the changes will cost and what they will produce in revenue. If the price of beef were 70¢ per lb, it would pay to spend 50¢ more per cow in order to get the additional lb. of beef. However, a fat cow may mean a poorer hide, and it may be possible to get more beef only at the cost of a poorer hide. The marginal cost of beef would be $\frac{\Delta y'}{\Delta m}$ + a loss on hides. This problem still remains unsolved.

There are three possibilities: Where the proportions are variable, the problem cannot be solved; where one can be increased without increasing the other, the solution just described applies; and where one can be increased only by decreasing the other, no solution has been found.

In order to decide a joint cost problem, it is necessary to know both costs and prices. After four or five years of trying to find from both economists and accountants, the solution was obtained from a mathematician who showed that it was a problem in multiple correlation.

July 21, 1930

In the case of electric current, if it is a case of producing more current, it is not a joint cost problem; but if one industry uses the current at night and another in the daytime, then it is a joint cost case. In the case of electric current, the timing of the use varies for different uses.

Monopoly Price

So far, we have been discussing something like perfect competition and in the textbooks they proceed to a discussion of complete monopoly. A discussion is sometimes seen as to whether or not there is more monopoly than competition. What is actually found is a form of competition not working out completely, or a form of monopoly adulterated with forms of competition. One rarely finds the types described in economic theory. Even in government agencies, there are elements of competition. Directors usually see the signs of competitive pressure first.

There is competition in buying, the factors used, at least. There is always competition for a place on the consumer's budget. Competition may not exist altogether, but there may be local arrangements in which there may be an appreciable influence resulting from the operation of a single producer. Where there are only a few producers in the industry and there is an inertia in finding a new consumer, the individual producers in the industry do have some effect on the markets. Even though a rival mill lowers its prices, a mill will hold its own customers, at least for a while. The system that we have is one in which there are substantial elements of both, and the most monopolistic elements face important competitive pressure, and in which there are a few types of industries in which the individual producers are not free to some extent from a type of inevitable price force. The theory of monopoly price means perfect monopoly, and this means 100 percent control of output.

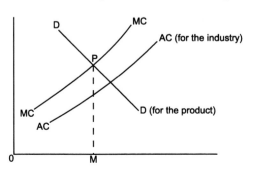

The cost of production must be kept in the picture, because it is one of the factors determining the monopoly price. The monopolist wants to maximize his excess of revenue over expenditure.

Suppose you cumulate or aggregate the *AC* curve in order to get an aggregate expense curve.

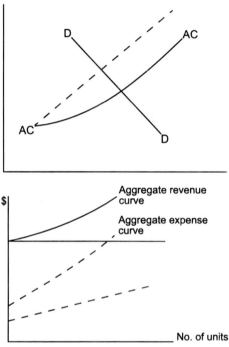

With an elasticity of less than unity, it would be a negative curve. The demand curve is always more negatively inclined than the aggregate revenue curve.

The following is another solution:

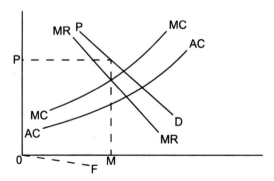

The marginal increments or the first differences of the cumulative curves should be secured. A marginal revenue curve should be drawn so that any point on this curve represents an increase of revenue obtained from an increase of 1 in sales. *MR* now becomes the significant curve for the determination of price. Any point on the *MC* curve represents an increase in aggregate cost resulting from an increase of one in output. At *OM*, the increase in marginal cost is just equal to the increase in marginal revenue. This is the point of equilibrium. It is still necessary to find the monopoly revenue price. If the vertical line from *M* is extended to the demand curve, this is the monopoly revenue price. Any point on the marginal revenue curve represents the increase in revenue from a sale of one more unit. If the demand has an elasticity of unity, the marginal revenue curve is a horizontal line. The change in revenue is zero. If the demand curve has an elasticity of less than unity, if it is highly inelastic, the marginal revenue curve will be below the base line (*OF*). The less elastic the demand curve, the greater the inducement to the establishment of monopoly. If it were less than unity, the maximum revenue output would be the smallest salable unit. If the elasticity were less than unity, any increase in output means a decrease in revenue. Under these circumstances, unless there is a cost curve of the particular character such that the greater the output the less the aggregate costs, it follows that, if the demand has an elasticity of less than 1, the fewer the units which are produced, the better off is the producer, and the optimum output is the smallest salable unit.

There are not many long-run elasticities less than unity. The general tendency, however, is to think that low elasticities are quite common. Most price situations are between this perfect monopoly and perfect competition. Partial monopoly is in between these two possibilities.

There is the problem of dealing graphically with the problem of partial monopoly. This is the case where there are concerns competing with each other, but one concern is important enough so that its changes in output exert an appreciable influence on price. There may be a concern in the industry that has about 45 percent or 50 percent of the productive capacity of the total industry, and there may perhaps be twenty-five other small producers. It is a follow-the-leader industry. One concern issues the price list, and the other concerns believe that the costs of price competition are too great to fight the large concern. The large concern, therefore, sets the price for the industry. How shall the leading factor find the price that it can charge on the principle of maximum revenue to it?

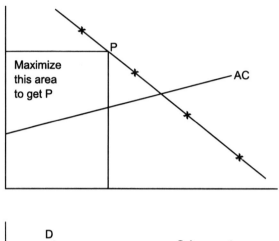

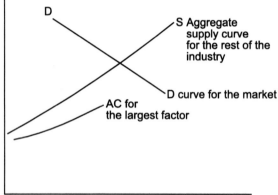

The individual concern has only a fraction of the total output, but it controls enough of it to influence the price significantly and it will find it to its interest to operate as a monopoly concern. It arranges its output according to the price.

This is the most important of the equilibrium graphs in terms of conditions as they are in industrialized countries. Most of our problems are problems in partial monopoly. As the percentage of the industry that the firm controls falls below 50 percent, the advantages of acting as a partial monopoly instead of as a competitive concern shrink very rapidly. Some advantage exists as long as it is a significant factor in the industry. This explains why several decades ago large American concerns tried to get control of 80–90 percent of the product. They found that the cost of getting control of the last units of the output was very great and aroused great legal and public opposition. They found that they still could oper-ate as a partial monopoly.

The clearest-cut case is where a large concern has several small competitors and it is known what the small competitors can produce. The supply curve for the others must be subtracted from the demand curve for the factors as a whole. This is also the problem of dumping under partial monopoly, which is the usual dumping situation. It is a problem in regional price discrimination.

For a monopoly, there is no distinction between internal and external economies. A monopoly can get the maximum possible advantage from economies of size, regardless of whether they are internal or external. Certain types of external economies may be lost by the monopolist, such as the cross-fertilization of ideas.

The net economies of monopolistic organizations are quite clearly distinguishable from economies of size. These are the elimination of competitive waste, such as competitive advertising. They would be a function only of the centralized control of the industry. There are many types of competitive waste, an example of which is the case of six milkmen operating in the same block.

Suppose that you were a government investigator trying to discover the existence of monopoly. You are looking for objective indicia or stigmata. What aid could price theory give you in identifying or getting clues as to the existence of monopoly?

1. Suppose you found a horizontal straight line in historical economic phenomena. Then, you ought to suspect pretty tight control, whether the straight line is the rate of output or the actual price or any other phenomena. A straight line is not only suspicious, it is eloquent. The packers, when confronted with this situation, argued that the stability of large numbers caused the straight line. There is no probability in the argument that two large aggregates in the same field shall run along precisely in the same way because of the stability of large numbers.
2. The most obvious argument for the existence of monopoly is that the price rises more sharply than for the competitive industries. The existence of monopoly is not the same thing as the existence of a high price. Under monopoly, the monopolist may find it to his interest to make the price lower than under competitive conditions. The monopolist can then get the important economies of large-scale production, and there may be important net economies of monopoly.
3. Uniformity of prices is an evidence of either perfect competition or monopoly. Since perfect competition is impossible, a price that is exactly the same for all producers is a sign of control or of inertia. Sluggish competition will also produce this result under certain circumstances.

In the case of the steel industry, there may be no agreement whatsoever, although a case might be made out that there is a tacit understanding. So far as absolute uniformity of prices is concerned, it is known that there is not a well-organized competitive market. Price competition operates through price differentials. If there were no price differences, competition could still work but not through price. Absolute uniformity of price can be established through absolute monopoly control as well as through sluggish competition.

Very little has been done on the statistical objective study of prices in terms of the types of organizations of the industry.

Notes

1. Ed.: W.F. Lloyd (1834).
2. Ed.: Edgeworth (1881), Fisher (1892), Davenport (1910), and Wicksteed (1910).
3. Ed.: Cournot (1838).
4. Ed.: Henry Ludwell Moore (1914) and Henry Schultz (1928).
5. Ed.: Justus von Liebig.
6. Ed.: A.C. Pigou (1920).
7. Ed.: Thomas Perronet Thompson (1826).
8. Ed.: F. Y. Edgeworth (1911).
9. Ed.: Léon Walras (1874) and William Stanley Jevons (1871).
10. Ed.: Frank A. Fetter (1915).
11. Ed.: Phillip Wicksteed (1910) and Herbert Davenport (1910).
12. Ed.: S. M. MacVane (1890), James Laurence Laughlin (1887), and J. Shield Nicholson (1893).
13. Ed.: Friedrich von Wieser (1892).
14. Ed.: Frank W. Taussig (1919).
15. Ed.: Horace Secrist (1924).

Second Term

Senior and McCulloch were the principal exponents of the wage-fund theory.[1] There are two paragraphs in J. S. Mill on the wage-fund theory, but the theory plays no vital part in his system. Thornton was the economist who made Mill recant on this point.[2]

In economic theory, we usually speak of the quantity demanded at a given series of prices. We should speak of the quantity demanded per week or per day. We should give our demands and supplies as rates of flows for a given period of time.

Miss Martineau tried to put economics into stories. If you want to see classical economics in its most rigid aspects, you will find it in Miss Martineau's *Illustrations of Political Economy*.[3] Miss Marcet's books are better, however.

The wage-fund theory never played a very important part in the doctrines of any economists except with respect to one issue where it seemed to be a plausible answer. That is with respect to the possibilities of collective bargaining and a sudden increase in wages as the result of a demand by labor.

For purposes of wage theory, the wage-fund theory was never of any importance. It is more important for interest theory, however. Only recently have economists kept clear the difference in amount of money and the amount of goods which can be measured by that amount of money.

The wage-fund theory was that at any one time the stock available for the payment of wages was a definite stock which was inelastic over short periods. If wages were high, unemployment would result; if wages were low, more laborers could be employed. If for the moment wages were low, there would be competition among the employers and they would bid up wages. If laborers were being paid more than could be paid and yet hire all the labor, there would be competition among the unemployed for jobs and wage rates would fall to a necessary equilibrium. The wage rate times the number of laborers should equal the subsistence fund. No matter how much wages are raised, the number of laborers who get employed is proportionately reduced. On the assumption of collective bargaining, allowance would have to be made for variations in the number of employed.

By the time of J. S. Mill, the wage-fund theory was a carry-over that had no particular function to perform in the system of distribution.

The essential feature of the theory is that wages are paid out of a past fund which cannot be increased nor decreased. Mill at one point, however, said that the fund could be decreased through export. The capitalist had to get an adequate return to his capital or he would export his capital, his wage fund. In this way, it is possible to drive a wage fund out of the country.

Fawcett was one of the last gasps of the wage-fund theory. In the 1870s, he criticized the exportation of capital from England on the grounds that it decreased the capital available for English labor.

What is wrong with the argument of Henry George that because there were high wages in a new area, there must be a lot of capital? What is the basis of measurement? A lot of capital wears a low interest rate relatively to the opportunities of using it profitably.

George contends that wages are paid out of the product. He overlooks, however, the lapse of time. The word "virtually" is almost always used to make something absurd sound sensible. The word is used in that way by George. He is trying to show that the creation of value and the payment of wages are simultaneous. The payment of wages may come after the creation of value, because ordinarily the wages are paid after the creation of value. According to George, labor makes an addition to the capital fund as soon as it withdraws its wages. George overlooked that what the labor adds is different in form from what it subtracts. Labor adds unfinished goods and subtracts finished goods. There is a pile of completed goods and another pile of goods in process. The laborer adds to the second pile and draws from the first. George gives the example of a pipe into which the laborer is pouring value and from which he is drawing wages. What the laborer puts in at one end of the pipe, however, is not what he takes out at the other end. If the putting in is stopped, that doesn't stop you from finishing the goods that have already been started.

The wage contract is a contract whereby the employer gives the employee a command over finished goods and whereby the employer gets from the employee his assistance in carrying on unfinished goods to a higher stage of production. To the extent that laborers save their wages, they free themselves from the wage-fund theory.

The wage-fund theory was a theory as to the extent of the limitation of real wages. You can vary the wage fund by varying the rate of spending or saving.

July 29, 1930

What is the wage fund on a certain date? The wage fund for 1931 on January 1, 1931 would consist of goods at any stage of completion consistent with being made ready for consumption within one year—goods of a sort suitable for consumption by the laborers. Some of the wage fund for 1932 would already be existing on January 1, 1931. A road excavator might be part of the wage fund for 1940. It might be but a factor in the bringing into existence of wheat, which would be available for real wages.

What percentage change in the size of the wage fund upward or downward would be made because of an increase or a decrease in the productivity of labor? It is possible to speed up the productivity of labor at its latter stages. Any suggestion of paying the labor out of an increased product is superficial because the increased product does not appear immediately in the form in which wages can be paid.

In connection with the problem of how real wages can be increased as quickly as the productivity of labor can be increased, the following should be noted:

1. It is possible to shift productive resources from the early stages to the more advanced stages of manufacture. Labor might be shifted from tending sheep to converting wool into cloth and cloth into garments. There would have to be a stock of wool on hand, in order to make this possible.
2. It is possible to make encroachments on the normal stock.
3. If labor voluntarily increases the amount of wages accepted in the form of promises to pay in the future, or that it reinvests immediately, the money wages can represent an increase in real wages. Provided they are not used, you can increase real wages by deferring the payment of a part of the wages by giving the laborers promises to pay or by giving them cash wages and by having them promptly reinvest their wages.
4. It is possible to divert to the consumption of labor commodities which would otherwise have been consumed by other classes. To a large extent, the rich and poor consume the same commodities in this country.

5. It is possible to divert some of the consumption that, in the physical sense, the other classes would themselves have consumed. This is possible to a greater extent than used to be the case.
6. Another way to quickly increase the real wages when the productivity of labor increases is by borrowing consumers' goods from abroad.
7. It is possible to shift unspecialized goods from use as producers' goods to use as consumers' goods. It is possible to use coal for heating a house or for driving a locomotive.

There is no difficulty in this problem if the number of laborers to be hired is variable. The number of laborers employed can then be reduced. The Classical School, however, had in mind an equilibrium situation in which all forces were employed.

The wage-fund theory was a short-run wage theory and most economists, therefore, paid very little attention to it. They used it as an answer to trade unionism in showing how wages could not be raised.

Items of flexibility in the wage fund are quite sufficient to take care of any problem of adjustment of wages paid such as is likely to occur. It is not possible to have productivity increased 20 percent over night. Within the limits of changes in productivity, there is no practical difficulty because of the fixity of the wage fund.

An increase in money wages would, to some extent, be absorbed by an increase in the prices of things that labor buys. This would be a short-run phenomenon. In the long run, the Classical School accepted the flexibility of the wage fund. It would and could be changed, and changes in productivity would be one of the things changing it. In the long run, they would have agreed that labor is paid out of its product. In the long run, there tends to be an equilibrium between the productivity of labor and its rate of return. The wage fund played no part in their long-run analysis.

Francis Amasa Walker was one of the outstanding American economists prior to the modern age. For the United States, he was as good as economics was in the United States at that time. He had a few theories that caught the attention of better economists than himself. He was important in reorganizing the American census on a proper basis. He was a good college administrator and had a colorful career. From 1890 to 1900, Walker's *Advanced Course* was probably the most popular college text, with J. S. Mill's *Principles* still competing to some extent.[4]

There were not many good economists in America before Walker. There were a few, however, of pretty good quality. One of these was McVickar. Raquet was a good monetary and banking theorist in the

1830's and 1840's. He was as good as any of the English theorists of his time.[5]

Vethake was an expounder of English Classical economics. He had no originality, however. Simon Newcomb was an independent original economist. He was primarily an astronomer. John Rae was not an American, although he lived in the United States for a short time.[6]

One of the reasons why Walker has been prominent is because it was quite a revelation to find that there was an American who could compete with the Continental economists and introduce concepts and ideas which they would accept.

Walker called his wage theory a "residual wage theory." Wages are the residual claimant of the product of labor. The marginal entrepreneur lives on what he could get if he worked for someone else. He had a demand and supply theory of interest without examining either the demand or supply. At one point, he says that interest will be determined by competent causes. Is there not a vicious circle in Walker? Does Walker show how profits can be determined independently of what the wage rate is, and is he not in the same difficulty with regard to rent?

July 30, 1930

Walker's theory is that if there is any change in productive conditions, labor will get the residual share. An unappropriated improvement which does not give special claims to one of the other parties will go to labor. Claims are made according to who is responsible for the increased production. Who the originator is does not matter unless he can make private property out of his idea.

Taussig says that, at the margin, there are no profits. Interest is determined by demand and supply and rent by no-rent land, and that leaves wages. Is that not Walker's theory? Taussig says that Walker uses circular reasoning. He says that there are no pure profits under pure equilibrium. He disposes of interest independently of wages. He finds that there is a constant rate of interest. You do not have to know what wages are to know what it pays to pay in interest. You may take it as fixed for purposes of distribution theory.

Taussig says that the effective rate of accumulation causes a constant rate of interest. This goes back to J. S. Mill and the Classical School's effective rate of accumulation. It has remained alive in Taussig's *Principles* as a pretty definite psychological rate of time preference. He says that over most of the range of possible savings, the time preference curve is a horizontal line, as follows:

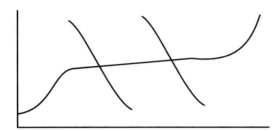

According to Taussig, time preference curves are flat. He has empirical evidence of this fact. He says that the rate of interest has remained constant as compared with wages in the last one hundred years

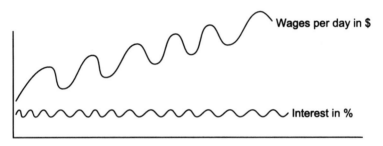

The above chart of Taussig's has not been published. It shows that there are only minor fluctuations in the interest curve with fluctuations about a central point. There are short-run fluctuations in the interest rate, but if one waits two or three years, savings will catch up and in this way, the effective rate of accumulation determines the rate of interest.

In the above chart, there are two independent scales. If the wage rate could be converted to an index number and charted on the wage scale, the mode of comparison would then be satisfactory. It would be found that the amplitude of fluctuations measured by the extent of year-to-year fluctuations has been much greater for interest than for wages. Interest fluctuates more from year to year than does wages. The interest rate and the wage rate must be placed on a chart on which they are reduced to comparable scales. Wages would be found to have a definite upward trend since the eighteenth century, whereas interest would not be found to have had such an upward trend. Since the nineteenth century, the general tendency of interest has been downward. There is no clear trend in interest over a long period of time. In the last 150 years, it is difficult to see any decided trend in either direction in the interest rate. Various factors affecting the interest rate have moved so that they have neutralized or offset each other.

The interest rate is much less stable than the wage rate. There is no force in the empirical evidence which Taussig used. Taussig has failed also to settle the interest rate independently of wages. Supposing one grants that Taussig has solved an independent rate of interest, has he gotten out of this circular reasoning? Taussig has been overlooked in Walker and, therefore, in his own theory that what the no-rent land shall be depends on the prevailing rate of wages. Rent changes because wage rates change. The profitable margin of cultivation depends on what it is necessary to pay for the factors of production. What shall be the no-rent farm shall depend on what wages and interest cost.

Taussig says that you cannot distinguish a specific product of labor from a specific product of capital—that you cannot separate the portions, but that you can distinguish the portion attributed to labor-capital from the two combined. Taussig says that the proportions between labor and capital are fixed by the state of the arts. The problem is the same as with joint costs. If the products of the factors are necessarily fixed in their proportions, it is nonsense to try to separate the labor product from the capital product. It is possible, however, to vary the proportions between land and labor-capital.

The labor-capital product is discounted and that discounted product goes to labor. It is really the marginal product of labor-capital. Capital is paid at the current rate. The product is discounted at the current rate and the remainder goes to labor.

The state of the arts might mean the technological practices actually in use at the time or the actual range of the processes. Taussig confuses these meanings. There are three possibilities, as follows:

1. Obsolete practices, about which you know but which you do not use.
2. Practices you are actually following.
3. Practices you know about and do not use, but could use if you wanted to.

These possibilities give the state of the arts a much more flexible meaning than the meaning which Taussig gives it.

There is a definite amount of technological knowledge scattered over various places, and only a small fraction of this is in actual use. The business world makes its selection from this collection of technological knowledge, and it makes the selection which is presumably the most desirable from the profits point of view of the entrepreneur.

There is no fixed state of the arts. What shall be most profitable depends on the prices of the factors. Change the rent or the interest and the financially permissible combination is changed.

Taussig's theory is a successive determination theory. Both Walker and Taussig have essentially the same theory of distribution. The difficulty with both is that you do not know where to start. It is impossible to find a part of the dividend which is determined prior to the determination of the other parts.

July 31, 1930

What does Taussig discount in his discounted marginal productivity formula? Hadley said that wages were the discounted product of labor before Taussig did, but he did not use the word "marginal."[7] For instance, take the product of a mill. It is a no-rent mill and there are no profits. There is the problem of separating the remainder into two portions of interest and wages. What is to be subtracted from that going to wages?

The discounting is on waiting that has already been done. The laborer gets the immediate value of his product. The laborer gets the value of the wheat he grows, but that is not the same as the value of the bread that will be made out of the wheat. There is a backward discounting. The payment for past advances and the reward for waiting have still to be done. The latter comes out of the difference between the present value of the product and the value it will eventually have. Labor and capital get all the present value of the product. It is already a discounted value, but there has been waiting in the past by capitalists and from this product of wheat, for instance, there will have to be subtracted [an amount] sufficient to pay interest on the capital borrowed in order to advance the previous wages. Out of the value of the wheat would have to come the wages of the agricultural laborers growing the wheat, the wages of the men who made the plow used in raising the wheat, old wages, and the interest on the advances which have been made to the laborers growing the wheat, assuming that they have been paid while the wheat was being raised, and also the interest on the advances in connection with making the plow and buying the plow, perhaps on credit.

What is discounted, according to Taussig, is the selling price of the product of labor cum capital. In the long run, the exceptions must work out exactly on average.

J. B. Clark speaks of natural wages.[8] With Clark, natural wages sometimes means wages under static equilibrium. At other times, it means competitive wages in a static competitive equilibrium. "Natural" also means "resulting from the action of the native impulses of man." Clark assumes that under competition and static equilibrium, a natural wage would result from men acting selfishly.

"Natural" here is essentially the "natural" of the Classical School. It is what we mean by "normal" these days. "Normal" was substituted for "natural" by Cairnes in about 1860.[9]

Clark's static state is the first elaborate exposition of a static state in English economics. The problem is, what would be the rate of wages if labor and capital remained fixed in quantity, if improvement in the mode of production stopped, if consolidation of capital were to cease, and if the wants of consumers were never to alter. This is a balanced aquarium idea in which there is no change from the outside.

Neoclassical economics is static, but it is not so static as Clark. In the case of Clark, all things are kept constant. In the ordinary neoclassical economics, everything but one factor is kept constant, and you see what consequences follow upon the change in the one factor. These two types of assumptions lead to different types of thinking.

Suppose you have a perpetual motion machine that is in motion. How is it possible to find out what wheel causes what wheel to turn? Is it possible to find an order of events?

$$a$$
$$b$$
$$a$$
$$b$$
$$a$$
$$b$$

It is necessary to know whether or not a precedes b. There is a time lag between the intervals. Is a the cause of b or is b the cause of a? It is impossible to tell from purely empirical observations. Where there are no irregularities, it is impossible to tell which is cause and which effect.

In Clark, there is a close approximation to what the Mathematical School developed before Clark wrote. Clark does not adhere consistently to a purely static hypothesis. He does not distinguish in his own mind the fundamental difference between his method of approach and that of Marshall's. This difference in method may explain the apparent difference in conclusions.

Clark uses the term "specific productivity." This is not just the same as "marginal productivity." In using "specific productivity," there is a difference in metaphysical significance. The marginal productivity theorist says merely that if you add one unit of labor to a given combination of factors, there will follow a given change in output, and this increment will be what labor will get per unit as its wage.

$$abc.... = x$$

$$abcd... = x+1$$

The marginal theorist does not want to be understood as saying that d in the above caused the "+ 1." He will say that the increase will be imputed to the addition of the factor d. He leaves the question of creation to those who are interested in it. Clark goes beyond this and argues that the particular factor d created the unit "+ 1." It is possible, according to Clark, to divide the product of wheat and to assign to both labor and capital its specific productivity.

$$a \text{ land} + b \text{ labor} + c \text{ capital} = m \text{ bushels}$$
$$a + 1 \text{ land} + b \text{ labor} + c \text{ capital} = m + n \text{ bushels}$$

There is an incremental change in output resulting from or accompanying an incremental change of 1 in labor. Clark means that when to a given situation you add a marginal increment of labor, you will get the increment it specifies of the product. Clark makes the n the specific product of the unit of labor and makes $(a + 1)n =$ the specific product of labor as a whole. It is an easy step from that sort of thing to make labor responsible and to be credited with that portion of the total output which would be assigned to it. With Clark, the emphasis is on the responsibility of the factor for the product.

Clark's theory is a theory both of metaphysical productivity, of causal responsibility for the factors as a whole, and of ethical justification of his system of distribution. Creation and responsibility are metaphysical notions. Finding the process of imputation is a legitimate scientific enterprise. Finding out whether the imputation is in accordance with creation is not of interest to economists. It is also an impossible task, because no answer can be found. All we can know is that an incremental change in a results from an incremental change in b. The breaking-up that we do is by imputation.

August 1, 1930

According to Clark, specific productivity means that to each agent goes his share of production. Clark thought of the system as a just and right system. If he were determined to deny the ethical implication, he could show that he was appraising it on the assumption that you accept certain standards. It is on the basis of consistency with the principle of private property that he is discussing distribution. It is based on the principle that men shall be paid according to their productivity. Property right does not rest only on creation, but on contract as well. He is not discussing legal right, but is discussing ethical right under the assumption that production has an ethical, valid claim to ownership under private property. Private property does not rest on the productivity principle as its prior principle. It rests on certain legal rights resting on contractual obligation. You may hire laborers to dig an oil well, and the well may produce nothing. You still have to pay the laborers.

Henry George said that the rate of wages was set by what squatter labor earned in the West. By a "squatter," he meant a farmer on no-rent land. Clark agreed with George but said that this was a temporary situation. Clark said that the squatters were getting not simply wages; they were getting wages plus an unearned increment. Workers in the city must get an equal income, which will consist of marginal productivity of their labor plus another addition to offset the unearned increment of the squatters. If a large percentage of the people were drawn out of the city, the marginal productivity of the laborer in the city would rise and wages would, therefore, rise. Finally the income of the two classes would be equal. The income in the city would be raised to the level of the country by raising the marginal productivity of the city workers.

Squatters get less immediate income than urban dwellers because they do not get their unearned increment at once, but they do get increasing land values, or hope to get them. What they do is to accept lower wages than those in the city in return for a prospect of getting some rent. During this period, they sell their products at lower prices, because of the expectation of securing the unearned increment.

The squatters probably do not get, in the long run, more than urban labor. They get land values only by giving their products to urban dwellers at lower prices, so that urban dwellers get a share of the squatter's unearned increment. The share of the urban laborer in unearned increment comes in high real wages and low prices rather than just in high wages.

Clark presents a marginal productivity theory of distribution and presents it in terms of a marginal field for labor consisting of a number of elements. These elements consist of all the possibilities for the marginal employment of labor. Supposing there is an influx of labor and there is the question of where employment can be found for them.

1. They can work on rent land more intensively.
2. They can be employed on no-rent land.
3. They can use poor instruments, instruments which had been ready to go to the scrap heap.
4. They can be employed by the more efficient working of good instruments or the more intensive use of good instruments.

By "efficiency," we mean efficiency in the use of some one factor. The engineer does not always remember that his formula is in terms of some one factor. "Efficiency" is rarely used by an economist in any real sense.

The extensive margin consists in working the additional labor on no-rent land and in using it on no-rent instruments other than land. The intensive use applies to the no-rent use of good instruments, including land. The zone of indifference is a limit within which men may go without affecting the employer's pocket. It is a limit within which it is of no appreciable difference to the employer whether men work or not.

Clark makes a distinction between capital and capital goods. The instruments are the capital goods. The capital goods are the concrete instruments and the capital is the value embodied in them. Capital is the pecuniary aspect and capital goods are the physical aspect.

There is an additional field for the employment of an influx of labor. This is the no-rent use of capital as distinguished from the no-rent use of capital goods. This involves a marginal transformation of stocks of goods into a new form. The capital shall be adjusted to a stock of labor larger by one unit than it had been before. This is a technological adjustment. Clark says that the zone of indifference give a limited field for the employment of additional labor, but this item is indefinite in extent. There is a readjustment of capital goods so that they shall be appropriate to the amount of labor available to work with them. This occurs through a process of replacing depreciated equipment. It would depend on the rate of depreciation of the particular concrete capital good.

If the general rate of wages rises, many instruments will be thrown out of use. They will have been no-rent instruments before and they now become instruments which it does not pay to use at all.

Wages are the marginal and specific product of labor. The marginal productivity of labor is the product at the zone of indifference. At the zone of indifference, there is no interest because no-rent instruments are being used, or you are making no-rent use of good instruments. There are no profits in the static state. You are left with labor entitled to that it produces and getting all the products at the zone of indifference.

Where the zone of indifference shall be shall depend on the wage rate. Also, what instruments shall be no-rent instruments shall depend on the wage rate. Labor gets what it can produce with no-rent instruments. Here, there is a vicious circle. This is another case of a residual theory where you have taken rent out by putting it in the class with capital and taken interest out by saying that labor uses no-rent instruments; labor gets all it produces, and what it produces is its own specific productivity and is what it gets. This is the same sort of circle as in Taussig and Walker.

Clark is an expounder of the marginal productivity theory. He was somewhat of a pioneer in expounding it. He worked out his marginal productivity theory for himself, while it had been already worked out in pretty good form. The theory was fairly well stated by von Thünen in Germany in the 1830's and 1840's and by Longfield in England in 1833.[10]

August 4, 1930

The appropriate first step in stating the marginal productivity theory is in terms of a universal law of diminishing returns. This is the law of labor-capital doses as applied to land. The marginal productivity of the increased factor will be equal to the increase in the total output from a marginal increase in that factor. As you increase one factor, leaving the others constant, the marginal productivity decreases with the product of the early factors becoming part of the product available for distribution.

It is necessary to postulate variable proportions between the factors. It is necessary to postulate that there are no fixed coefficients, that there are no factors which enter into the production in such a way that the unit of a factor necessary for a unit of output is necessarily the same. The amount of a factor in a particular product is not fixed, or, even though fixed as an economic cost, the question as to how much of it shall be involved in waste depends on its price plus the price of the factors to be used in extracting it. It is impossible, therefore, to suggest fixed coefficients.

One argument made against the universality of the law of diminishing returns is that the proportions between labor and capital are fixed by the state of the arts. Taussig subscribes to this more or less, and Laughlin still subscribes to it.

In the short run, the possibilities of varying the factors are limited, but, nevertheless, there is a fairly substantial degree of variability even in the short run. There are these broad classes of possibilities:

1. The use of the same technique, the same "state of the arts," but with a double-shift or overtime, or half-shift or short time, or with more labor for the same machine, or more labor per acre. In any factory, it is possible to speed up the rate at which a conveyor carries the work to be done past the workers. You can change the unit of the factors for the plant as a whole or for a unit of the product. You can use the capital in varying proportions for the twenty-four-hour day.
2. You can make use of a different known technique. This requires a different proportion of labor to capital. When the form of the capital goods is changed, this takes some time. It is impossible to do this more rapidly than the rate of depreciation of existing investment.
3. Even though the proportions of the factors remain the same, in every single industry, you can, nevertheless, change them for the industry as a whole by shifting the factors, say from an industry in which labor is unimportant to one in which labor is important. The price factor might make it profitable to make such a shift. Capital would become high, and labor cheap, and products that use little labor and much capital would become dear. With the shift to the other type with labor being drawn in and capital being diverted, in that way there could be a labor-capital redistribution for the industries. This also requires time and it cannot be carried on more rapidly than the rate of depreciation plus the amount of the growth factor. Its maximum is not over 10 percent per year.

These three factors as listed above are probably sufficient to give very nearly all the flexibility that is necessary for approximate adjustment.

I think it is fair to say that the marginal productivity theory was a big and complex body of doctrine before the marginal productivity stage. It is something like the standard doctrine of the 1890's with the marginal productivity element added to it. The marginal productivity theory is only one phase of the system. Men are labeled by the designation of the most modern accretion to their doctrines. The marginal productivity theorist may also be a utility theorist. He may accept a good part of classical and neoclassical doctrine. This theory was applied in the doctrine of the classical and neoclassical schools.

If it is an ethical theory, it must be remembered that you do not develop ethical doctrines for the idiot. An ethical doctrine of praise and blame and of reward and punishment implies a measure of free will and power to determine for oneself what one's actions shall be. The same holds true for legal responsibility.

What does the marginal productivity theory actually say in terms of labor? Here, some differences make their appearance such that the conventional classification of the factors does have some practical significance at this point. Previous to this time, everything said would also apply to rent profits and interest.

What does the marginal productivity of labor depend on? In so far as it is beyond his will, the laborer is not entitled to high wages for high productivity and vice versa on ethical grounds.

The following are the things that might make the marginal productivity different:

1. Efficiency of the management.
2. Type of capital goods.
3. The supply curve of labor, its position, and its elasticity.
4. The public goods available in the form of government action, service to the industry, etc., plus the cultural inheritance of technology which no individual can appropriate for himself.

For all these things the laborer is not responsible. There are, however, some personal elements left. It is impossible, however, to blame him for lack of physical strength on account of malnutrition, ill fortune, or accidents. You are left with a residual of individual factors, i.e., whether he is lazy or industrious, whether he is faithful, and whether he tries to learn. You cannot blame an individual for the supply curve of labor.

On marginal productivity grounds, there is little basis for praising labor for its high marginal productivity or to attribute to its own lack, its low marginal productivity. The personal element is only one element of many. The other factors are of greater potential importance, and it is not a matter on which you can easily get an ethical justification of the present system by citing marginal productivity reasoning.

Labor	Aggregate Output going to Labor	Average Product Imputed to Labor	Price per Unit of Product
100 units	1,000 units	10 units	$2.00
250 units	2,000 units	8 units	$1.00

Under these conditions, the fall in the value of the product will be 20:12 because of the decline in price, instead of 10:8. This is reasonable only on the assumption that you are speaking for some particular kind of labor. It is impossible to reason thus for all labor, because there cannot be a fall in all values.

Supposing a situation in which you increase all labor by a given amount, everything else remaining the same except as it adjusts itself to this change. Changes in relative value will result. Some will go up in value and some will go down. An increase in the amount of one factor will lead to a shift in the relative values of commodities. The reasons for this shift will be that labor becomes cheaper, factors using relatively less labor will decline in cost of production and, therefore, in price as compared with products making relatively little use of labor. Different products use factors in different proportions.

The use by different products of factors in different proportions would have to be combined and taken in conjunction with the elasticity of demand for the different factors in order to find out just what types of change in relative prices would occur as a result of the change in the price of labor. It is necessary to know the relative elasticities of the demands of the factors. There would be changes in relative prices, because different factors spend their returns on different classes of commodities.

August 5, 1930

The following should be noted in connection with why an increase in the amount of labor in a country will change relative prices:

1. Different products use factors in different proportions, and their relative cost curves would change. They have demands of different elasticities, and the two combined would tend to produce a new system of relative prices.
2. The fact that different factors spend their returns on different classes of commodities would tend to disturb the existing system of relative prices. With an increase in the number of laborers in a country, let us assume that there are certain types of goods which the working classes tend to consume. Increasing the number of laborers ought to affect the demand for such commodities and, thus, to change their prices relative to the prices of other commodities.
3. Different commodities have different technical conditions of production; so that if there is a 10 percent increase in the amount of labor in the country and a decrease in wage rates and an absorption of more labor in each industry relative to the other factors, the diminishing

marginal productivity curve for labor will vary from industry to industry. In some industries where it is possible to add a lot of labor without reducing marginal productivity very much, a lot of labor will be absorbed and the output of such products will be increased much before it does not pay to use any more labor. There is a drop in physical productivity per laborer, a reduction in the wage rate, and a drop in the value per unit of product. These three elements must be equilibrated. The difference in the rate of slope of the productivity curve will be a factor in how soon the three-fold equilibrium will be reached, and equilibrium will be reached at points at which the relative prices will be different from what they were before. You get different sorts of results according to the slopes you assume for your marginal productivity curve of labor. If you assume that the marginal productivity curve has a slope of less than 1, an increase in the amount of labor would mean a decrease in the marginal productivity of labor. The aggregate product attributed to labor is less for a large stock of labor than for a stall stock. Labor would get less money income than before. There is probably no practical situation in which it is plausible to assume a marginal productivity curve with a greater slope than 1.

Let us assume that the marginal productivity curve is greater than 1 for labor; the measure of the slope is 1 plus. Supposing you increase the amount of labor in the country. The supply curve shifts to the right. These three propositions arise from the more general propositions already laid down:

1. It is more favorable if labor spends its income on products requiring relatively much labor for their manufacture. There will be a partial compensation to labor for the increase in the prices of the things they ordinarily consume, because much will go to labor.
2. The results will be more favorable to labor if the products requiring much labor for their manufacture have relatively high elasticities of demand. Articles requiring much labor are going to fall relatively in price. If products requiring much labor have high elasticities, a decrease in price means a large increase in demand. The value productivity of labor will not fall sharply because of the increase in the amount of labor.
3. The situation will be favorable to labor if products of the types consumed largely by labor and/or products requiring relatively much labor for their manufacture are produced in industries in which the diminishing productivity curves for labor have a relatively small inclination. If the measure of their slopes is high, the directions in which an increase of labor is likely to be most absorbed will be the directions in which the physical marginal productivity of labor will not fall sharply.

The question is, under what circumstances will the new situation of the individual laborer be best as compared with the old situation? Under what circumstances will the impairment be least? If you assume elasticities of less than 1, some of the above propositions would be directly reversed, or if you assume that labor spends its income on products using relatively little labor for its manufacture, these propositions would tend to be reversed.

The following objections have been made to marginal productivity theory of distribution on technical grounds:

1. It is a truism. There is an obvious identity between marginal productivity and wages. The answer to this objection is that other critics say that it is untrue. It cannot be both a truism and untrue, although some say that it is both. Logically it is possible for labor to get more or less than its marginal productivity. There is neither necessary nor logical identity between wages of labor and marginal productivity. The theory states that labor tends to get its marginal product. There would hardly be an exact equivalence at any one time. The theory explains why labor gets the marginal productivity, and it discusses the factors which determine what that marginal productivity shall be.
2. It is objected that the productivity of labor is not distinguishable or measurable, or that there is no separate product of labor. There is some disagreement within the ranks of marginal productivity theorists on this point. The J. B. Clark type has in mind a metaphysical concept of creation of productivity. The word "specific" is intended to imply this. The answer to this objection is that a properly stated marginal productivity theory makes no assertion as to ultimate metaphysical responsibility for the product. It is on its guard not to say anything about the metaphysical responsibility for the product.

The marginal productivity theorists say that what labor produces is the amount of aggregate product which will be imputed to labor. It is impossible to break up a product into that created by the several factors. It depends on the marginal events and the marginal productivity theorists assert merely what happens at the margins. As you change the working combinations, what society does on the basis of these marginal happenings is the important factor. This theory does not in any way commit itself to any statement as to what labor as a whole produces. It states only what changes occur at the margins as a result of incremental changes in the factors and alleges what the market does on the basis of these marginal changes. The best of the marginal productivity theorists is Wicksell, the Swedish economist.

I am not interested in knowing how much of the whole of a commodity is produced by free goods, land, labor, and capital. There is no way of finding an answer to that sort of a question. One should be interested only in the ethical aspect of it.

The facts of marginal change are undeniable. The actual process of distribution in a rational competitive society is also undeniable. Any departure of the entrepreneur from the marginal productivity system is a mistake for him.

There is also the argument that it is impossible to find marginal productivity. This is a variant of the above criticism. Hobson makes much of this argument.[11] He has been fighting the use of differential calculus throughout his economic career, and he stresses the indivisibility of the factors into sufficiently small units. In any field, the use of infinitesimals is to state things more clearly. The variations of the actual observations from the results to be detected if the units could be divided would follow no rule, and the only pattern in the situation would be the pattern that would be outlined in the solution along the line of infinitely divisible units. In most cases of large units, it is assumed that it pays to stop short of, rather than to go beyond, the point to be detected as the stopping point. The general tendency is to carry production and consumption less far than if the units could be infinitely divisible. Labor is divisible and capital is not divisible, but given time and in the long run it can be adjusted so that the new situation shall be just slightly different from the old one. Land, in the long run, is divisible.

So far as an ethical theory is concerned, on the basis of some doctrine of responsibility and of free will and free determination, labor is not largely responsible for what its marginal productivity is. Particularly, the individual laborer is not responsible. One of the factors in the conventional classification is not human at all, namely land.

Clark has never bothered to distinguish between the human element and the physical element. He has not raised the issue of ownership. The implication that reward should go to the owner or owners of the product is found in Clark. There is nothing in Clark's ethical implications contrary to the proposition that in a slave state, the productivity of the slaves belongs to the owner of the slaves.

There is another phase of marginal productivity theory as an ethical justification. Veblen pointed out the paradox that if you doubles the supply of labor, other things remaining the same, the gross product of industry will increase but the marginal productivity of labor will fall and the amount going to labor as wages may fall.[12] Veblen says "will fall." The marginal productivity system has neither direct nor immediate ethical implications. It is necessary to bring into the study, in addition to the economist's description of how it works, some fundamental notions of what is right and what is not right. This leads to the conclusion that there are only two ways in which labor can raise wages: (1) by reducing its numbers, and (2) through the development of personal efficiency.

Chapman's book is a routine explanation of Marshall.[13] It is a good book to go to if you are in difficulty of understanding Marshall.

The factors affecting the marginal productivity of labor are better management, improvement in the quality of the entrepreneur, batter distribution of technical knowledge, and more government aid. Almost any phase of the economic factors will tend to affect the marginal productivity of labor. Labor as a whole can work harder, or more efficiently, or decrease its numbers.

It has been said that the marginal productivity theory is capitalistic apologetics, because it implies the futility of trade unionism, and that it is a part of the general theory of demand and supply and of competitive price making. This assumes that it is a system in which employers compete with each other for labor and laborers compete with each other for jobs. The marginal productivity theory has little to say about the possibilities of collective bargaining. Collective bargaining is simply an agreement as to the price that will be given if any price is given at all. In collective bargaining, the employer is still free to deal with differentials. The number of laborers to be hired is not contracted for. The employer can still make differential or marginal adjustments.

The marginal productivity theory need not be applied to labor as a whole. It can be applied to any sub-classification that may be made. Any particular class of labor in any particular locality tends to get a wage equal to its marginal value product in that locality and for that classification.

August 6, 1930

So far as the demand for the factors is concerned, what the employer is looking for is some instrument that will do certain things for him and whether the agent is labor, land, or capital makes little difference to him. His engineers will design his plant so that it will use factors in different proportions without stopping to think of the substitutes.

On the supply side of labor, you are dealing with the feelings and the emotions of the particular people concerned. In a good deal of economic thinking, you can simply identify population and labor supply and assume that they are the same. Ordinarily population and labor supply go in the same direction. If the age distribution is more favorable and is such that there are more persons within the limits of working ages, the population may decrease but the working supply will increase. The proportion of the population within a range of years has nothing to do with the wage rate. The percentage of the population gainfully employed or within a conceivable range of working ages quite plausibly may depend on the prevailing scales of remuneration. The age at which children go to work and the age at which men and women retire from work may be dependent on the prevailing scales of remuneration. A change in the rate of remuneration might change the labor supply.

Assuming static analysis, a higher wage conceivably reduces or increases the amount of absenteeism, the number of days per week, or the average number of days that men shall work. The labor supply can be affected by changes in the length of the working day without changing the number of laborers. Properly defined, the labor supply is also a matter of the intensity with which labor is worked, or the rate at which they turn out output. This is obvious when laborers are paid on the piece-rate basis. The rate of remuneration may affect the intensity with which the men work. All of these are fairly short-run possibilities of adjustment of the amount of labor to the rate of remuneration. These factors would work to create a negative supply curve. It does not matter whether the curve is positive or negative; in either case, the Austrian assumption that there is a fixed supply of labor and a given amount of the various factors would be objectionable. It would lead to erroneous results in that there is an inclination in the supply curve of labor.

The view of the Mercantilists of the eighteenth century was that the supply curve seems to fall back in itself in terms of labor hours and intensity of work. If you put a Jamaican Negro to work on a banana plantation in Jamaica and were to pay him 10¢ per hour, and on this wage he could not get much to eat, he might work more hours if you paid him 20¢ per hour. At 10¢ per hour, he might not work at all; at 30¢ per hour, he might work longer. But if you were to give him 40¢ per hour, the wages of the last hour would be low for him and he would reduce the number of hours he would be willing to work. The curve of labor would be like the following one, which is found in Fisher[14]:

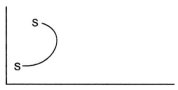

There is some reason for believing that the attitude of the eighteenth-century English laborer was something like the southern American Negro. It is the attitude of a people as yet undisciplined to the regular routine of labor.

During the Wilson administration, when the highest grades of railroad workers were threatening to strike and were demanding a high overtime premium for work over eight hours, I asked a railroad brotherhood man whether they wanted the longer hours with extra pay or whether they wanted the shorter day and, thus, wanted to create a punitive surtax. He said that the union was divided on this point. Some wanted one and some wanted the other.

The labor supply is given simply because there is at any one time a fixed amount of population. That does not mean that there is a given amount of labor regardless of the rate of remuneration. The Classical School had a long-run theory as to the relationship between wages and the amount of labor. The rate of increase of population was a function of the rate of wages. If the wage rate went up, marriages would take place at an earlier age, and there would be more children per marriage. Some economists indicated the positive checks of Malthus and stated that with higher wages, more children would survive. This is the subsistence level of wages. La Salle called it the "iron law of wages."[15] No English economist ever held this in this crude, rigid form, but Malthus was the closest to it. Ricardo made subsistence a conventional thing, a conventional standard of living. As soon as it becomes conventional rather than physical, the positive checks are out of the picture. This explains why there is no emphasis on the positive checks in discussions of English wage theory. Somebody has called La Salle's iron law of wages, the "brass law of wages."

Population responds positively and varies directly, although not proportionately, with the rate of remuneration of labor. In the, long run, wages tend to equal the subsistence level for labor. At any one time, population would determine the productivity, the margin at which land would have to be worked and, therefore, would determine the wage rate. In the long run, the requirement is that the wage rate must equal the standard of living. In the short run, the only requirement is that it shall be sufficient to take off all the existing labor.

In Adam Smith's discussion of differences in wages, is it his point that there is a charge for the inconstancy of the job so that the annual earnings will be larger for the worker? I suspect that he was thinking of the wage rate per small unit of time. Smith is also ambiguous in his discussion of the possibility of success. He did not mean the actual insurance premium for the chances of larger profits, but here, he is speaking in terms of net income per year. It is the mistakes in judgment that he seems to have in mind. He also speaks of the easiness and cheapness of learning an occupation. If the occupation is difficult to learn, the person learning it takes the strain and pays the cost. If it is expensive, it is generally the parents who bear this cost. In terms of pain costs, differences of wages are simply sufficient to allow for differences in the agreeableness of the different occupations. These are called "equalizing differences." These differences make the rates equal for the same expense of effort or disutility.

Does Smith say that all differences can be accounted for on the basis of attractiveness? Where there is a government monopoly on entrance into a given occupation, this might explain a difference. Assuming no government monopoly, what is the relation of trust? Presumably, a man who can excite trust in himself can get higher pay. Is it his point that men who can excite trust are a sort of natural monopoly? Again, he is ambiguous. Probably he thought of it as something people do not like and, therefore, desire higher pay for assuming the position involving trust. Smith places his emphasis on equalizing the differences. Differences in the attractiveness of the occupation are most important.

J. S. Mill added that there is not sufficient competition between the different occupations to equalize the differences and that you often see that the attractive, pleasant occupations are the highest paid ones.[16]

Karl Marx went furthest in the equalizing theory. With him, skilled labor was the equivalent of, for instance, 1.3 or 1.5 of ordinary labor. Cairnes gives us an explanation of his non-competing groups, of those groups whose relative remunerations need not be equalizing because entrance and exit to and from these groups is not free. Relative rates of remuneration are determined by relative scarcity of the numbers in the two groups in relation to the relative demands for their services. If there were free movement, it would be a condition of equilibrium that the rate of remuneration would be the same for both groups.[17]

Cairnes pointed out the existence of non-competing groups and used them to explain differences in wages. J. S. Mill had already explained "non-competing groups," but he did not use this term. Reputations are sometimes more easily made by originating a good term for an idea than by thinking of the idea. Cairnes survives in economics because of this one term, "non-competing groups." In the same way, Senior gets the credit for coining the term "abstinence." Cairnes held that it was not necessary that relative wages shall be as marginal disutility. The return is not according to effort, since there are monopoly elements in the different occupations.

(ECONOMICS 303)[18]

(1) $D_1 = F_1(p_1 \ldots \ldots ..p_n)$

$D_2 = F_2(p_1 \ldots \ldots ..p_n)$

. . . .

$D_n = F_n(p_1 \ldots \ldots ..p_n)$

D = amount taken; p = price to n = commodities

(1a) $D_1 = S_1$

$D_2 = S_2$

. . . .

$D_n = S_n$

(2) $F_1(p_1 \ldots \ldots ..p_n) = S_1$

$F_2(p_1 \ldots \ldots ..p_n) = S_2$

. . . .

$F_n(p_1 \ldots \ldots ..p_n) = S_n$

To produce one unit of article (n), it is necessary to use $a_n + a_{nr}$ of means of production". 1 to n = factors of production. Prices of means of production" = $q \ldots .. q_r$.

(3)   Cost of production function. The factors and technical coefficients are given, but the apportionment is to be determined among the industries:

$a_{(1)_1} q_{(1)} + a_{(1)_2} q_{(2)} + \cdots .. a_{(1)_r} q_{(r)} = p_1$

$a_{(2)_1} q_{(1)} + a_{(2)_1} q_{(2)} + \cdots .. a_{(2)_r} q_{(r)} = p_2$

. . . .

$a_{(n)_1} q_{(1)} + a_{(n)_2} q_{(2)} + \cdots .. a_{(n)_r} q_{(r)} = p_n$

(The above equations should be read in the following manner: A quantity of factor 1 necessary to produce a unit of commodity (1) times the price of factor 1, plus a quantity of factor 2 necessary to produce a unit of commodity (1) times the price of factor 2, etc.)

In Cassel, the monetary problem is left out.[19]

The United States tariff provides for 33,000 specific commodities, aside from grade differences. There are several hundred thousand distinct identifiable commodities of trade. A good many, however, have no practical significance on the price of any one particular article. Marshall made one step toward this in his beef-pork example. In taking account of five or six other commodities, you may be taking account of a good many others through reflection. Most economic phenomena can be almost wholly expressed in terms of six or seven of the important variables.

The commodities will have to take such prices as will make the amounts produced equal the amounts that the market is willing to take.

The amounts of the basic factors are fixed. The factors $1-r$ are fixed. Each one is fixed in amount, but what commodities they shall be used to produce is one of the things to be determined. The technology is fixed. There are constant costs, with neither external nor internal economies. There are no possible variations in the proportions of the factors as a fixed "state of the arts."

If there is an increase of labor in the country and the technical coefficients of production are fixed, shifts in prices will take care of this. The relative prices of the factors would change, and the factors using labor heavily would become relatively cheaper.

(4) Same as (1)

(5) $\quad D_{(1)} = S_{(1)}$

$D_{(2)} = S_{(2)}$

$D_{(n)} = S_{(n)}$

Statement of the total units of factor number 1 necessary to produce all amounts that are going to be produced:

(6) $\quad a_{(1)_1} S_{(1)} + a_{(2)_1} S_{(2)} + \cdots .. a_{(n)_1} S_{(n)}$

Of the means of production $^n r$, we need:

$a_{(1)_r} S_{(1)} + a_{(2)_r} S_{(2)} + \cdots .. a_{(n)_r} S_{(n)}$

$R_1 \cdots \cdots R_r = qu's$ available for means of production^n

$$(7) \quad R_1 = a_{(1)_r} \, s_{(1)} + a_{(2)_r} \, s_{(2)} + \cdots .. a_{(n)_r} \, s_{(n)}$$

Equation 3 gives the prices of the products. If one knows the prices, he can get the amounts that would be bought from Equation 4. Knowing the amounts that would be bought, equation 5 will give the amounts that will be produced. The amounts of each factor will be obtained from equation 6. Equation 7 would guarantee that the amounts of the factors available would be the amounts used.

Conclusions from Cassel's equations:

1. The equations demonstrate that based on certain assumptions, you can count the unknowns and that you have a determinate problem and a determinate solution. They show the conditions under which you would have a definite mathematical solution of the problem if you had determinate functions.
2. The equations give you the scheme of interrelationships, the things that must equal other things in order for the system to be adjusted.
3. The equations do not show, however, what kind the relationship is. From these equations, men have drawn implications by assuming that these equations are of certain types.

What the equations do show is that the things are interrelated and that the problem may be determined. In the demand function, most of the prices of other commodities could be struck out, because they would have an effect of almost zero. But for a mathematically correct answer, you could not strike out anything. If you did, the conclusion could not be checked.

In these equations, marginal productivity is not taken care of. This is not an objection against the equilibrium school but against Cassel. He argues against the productivity theory to protect his equations.

Cassel assumes that the *qu*'s are unknown the longest. He does not take account of the dependence of the technique of production on the general situation. This shall depend on the prices of the factors. How many units of factors shall be available for use will also depend on the rates of remuneration and the prices of the factors. The technical coefficients are matters not only of the proportions of the factors but also of the scale of the industry. The technical coefficients will be a function of the relative prices of the factors.

There is also an omission of the dependence of the demand functions on the distribution of income. It depends also on the size of the income.

Walras and Cassel would assume constant employment. The demand function would depend on the amounts of the factors, and these factors would influence the amount of the income.

There is a group of Swedish economists at Stockholm who allege that Cassel's system does not take care of the interest problem and the time problem. They state that it is necessary to rewrite the whole system in a more complicated way to take care of the question of how long you have to keep a factor, also the value problem between immediate goods and partly finished goods, etc. There is also the question of the relation to disutility and utility theory. Does Cassel's theory take care of utility theory? The demand functions are dependent on utility functions, and this dependence is not shown. However, utility functions depend on customs, manners, and habits, and these depend on past history. It is not possible to get a complete system. It is necessary to start somewhere arbitrarily.

What is accepted as given is the amounts of the factors, and the demand functions. It has been argued that it is impossible to start with demand functions because of complicated utility functions. The farther back one goes, the less is the logical error.

In residual theories of distribution, an attempt is made to isolate the products of the different factors. Cassel's theory would discourage this sort of attempt on the ground that all factors have their shares determined simultaneously. All prices are determined simultaneously and are mutually dependent.

I am not aware of any theoretical influence in the treatment of any economic problem in this general type of approach. Men following this approach have maintained themselves on an abstract level, or if they have attached concrete problems, it is difficult to find how they are exponents of this sort of theory.

Pareto handled many points more sharply and better than many economists.[20] Cassel has not thrown any new light on any part of economic theory. Pareto met the criticism that you cannot measure utility schedules by going back to equivalence or choice or indifference curves. The indifference curve was invented by Edgeworth, and Pareto took it from him.[21] An indifference curve is a curve of equivalent pairs. Pareto worked with choices or preferences. He derives demand schedules out of these indifference curves or choices. His system starts with the idea that demands are the results of the exercise of choice and the technological conditions of production, which are, for him, variable. The range of choice of the combinations is given. What the right choice is will be settled at the same time.

Cassel points out that margins are settled only when you know what the equilibrium situation is. All margins are settled at the same time. One should not say that marginal cost determines price, but that marginal cost must equal price under conditions of equilibrium. Cost curves determine price. Demand schedules and utility schedules determine price.

Cassel's theory is that men save to take care of their future needs. They save in order to have more to spend later on. The shorter the probable duration of life, the less likely they are to save and the more likely they are to spend. This is one great flaw in Cassel's theory. He does not take into account the fact that people save for their children, which makes the probable duration of life of little consequence in affecting willingness to save. He takes 2 percent as the ratio between income from saving and from conversion to annuities. When income per year from converting into annuities gets to be twice as much as income from saving, men will stop saving. On that basis, you can calculate just at what interest rate men would convert capital into annuities, which are a compromise between capital and consumption funds. It is impossible for interest to fall below 2 percent. It would then pay them to convert their capital into annuities. Above 4 percent, it would pay them to convert earned income so far as possible into investment.

Cassel's theory does not take dependence into account. To get the ratio between earned and saved income, you have to have some idea of the probable duration of life. The longer the life, the lower the ratio of annuity income to investment income.

It can also be objected that the theory gives a wrong picture of the incentive to save. Cassel operates on the basis that men save to provide for their own consumption. It is necessary to add the interest of the dependents, which makes the probable duration of life an indefinite concept. When the duration of life is very long, the annuity proposition gets to be almost meaningless. People save not merely for themselves and their dependents. Saving may be a part of the process of building up a business. Building up a business is a pleasurable activity in its own right, one that engrosses the interest of the individuals engaged in it. It is a very important element in saving by the businessman. A large part of the motive is to make the business grow. It is the business rather than the saving that is the objective.

There is also institutionalized saving in the form of corporate saving. The corporate relationship between shareholders and the management of the corporation is sometimes as tenuous as the relationship between a voter and the government. The acts of a board of directors may have little relationship to the wishes of the shareholders in the matter of plowing back earnings. Only about 6 percent of the Canadian Pacific Railway is owned in Canada and yet its directors regard it as a Canadian institution. It is the second largest railroad in the world and yet located in a country of small population. Questions of the interest of Canada play a part in its operation, which would be of no interest to shareholders in England and Germany. Big corporations tend to reinvest. Business men tend to nourish a business instead of having the business nourish them. From 30 percent to 40 percent of net additions to invested capital in the United States takes the form of plowing back of earnings of corporations. What has this to do with the problem of the duration of life? Whose duration of life is it?

There is also the miser attitude or complex, which in extreme form is pathological. Traces are to be found in a larger percentage of mankind. It is based on a sense of accumulation and a sense of power.

There is also the saving that is purely habitual. Another factor is moral saving, of saving as a virtue. Luxury is a sin and leads to moral deterioration; therefore, saving is carried on in the belief that frugality and prudential action are virtues.

There is some inductive material tending to disprove Cassel. Censuses of wealth by age are scarce, but I have found a few:

Norway, 1911 (Actual Census)

Age	Income	Property
20	286 kr.	124 kr.
20–30	539 kr.	455 kr.
30–40	876 kr.	1,807 kr.
40–50	1,050 kr.	3,741 kr.
50–60	1,041 kr.	5,146 kr.
60–70	912 kr.	6,261 kr.
70+	738 kr.	7,532 kr.

Great Britain,1905

Age	Average Estate at Death
20	£749
20–25	1,164
25–35	1,161
35–45	2,195
45–55	2,650
55–65	3,650
65–75	4,714
75+	6,618

The institution of settlements should make the last three periods decrease the average estates. The wealth per estate for males in New South Wales rises steadily until the age group eighty to eighty-nine is reached. For the group over ninety, there is a big drop. This is partly caused by attempts to escape inheritance taxes and partly by the fact that by that time, the people are too weak to resist pressure.

Victoria shows similar results. Estates at death move up until the eighty to eighty-nine group is reached but drop after ninety. Estates of women, however, keep on rising even after ninety. They do not give up.

		Men	Women
New South Wales	80–89	4,773	3,234
Victoria	90 +	2,025	2,596

However, these are rather small areas with small populations and when you get a group of ninety and over, the statistical stability would be small. These figures conform to the proposition that the probable duration of life does not play a great part, because it does not induce men to convert their property into life annuities.

August 7, 1930

It does not follow that since there are noncompeting groups, particular costs or disutilities play no part in the determination of relative wages, but if you find that the rates of remuneration are in inverse correlation or negative correlation with the degrees of intensity or unpleasantness or difficulty of the occupation, you know that there are other factors in the situation which are more important working in the opposite direction. Comparative pain would be a minor factor in the situation. Nobody has really done any careful observing to try to see what effect the comparative attractiveness of an occupation has on its rates of remuneration. The higher the level of the class, the more interesting and the shorter seems to be the work they do. Apparently the deciding factors do not include comparative disutility. Supposing one investigates within one of those groups, he would find a range of occupations that seem to indicate quite substantial differences in the attractiveness of occupations within a group of this sort. Suppose one studies a big sample of an educated social group on a high social standing and studies the occupations that the sons of the families get into and in which they had been working for fifteen years. Suppose one were to study 10,000 of these individuals to see whether there was any correspondence between the groups and the attractiveness of the occupations. The correlation that one would expect to find would be as to ability rather than as to attractiveness of the occupation. There is theoretically a scope for the operation of comparative pains as an influence on wages. Nobody has done sufficient observing to justify expressing himself with any degree of confidence.

In the South African gold mines, the work on the surface and the work underground, from the point of view of skill and physical strength required, is about the same. Wages underground are about twice as high as on the surface. Any worker may choose between one and the other. The disadvantages of working underground are the intensity of the heat, the health factor, and the unattractiveness of working underground. Laborers are drawn from the same body and are transferable. This is a clear-cut case where comparative disutility is the significant factor in explaining the differences in the rates of pay of these two groups.

There is also a case in the electrical industry in which some men work on poles and some work on the ground. Another example is that of structural steel workers on bridges and skyscrapers. In about 1920, skilled structural steel workers were getting twice as much as those working near the ground. This may have been a noncompeting group in a sense, but a good many working on the ground did not work above the ground, because it was unattractive to them.

Comparative disutility of the occupations would still exert some influence on noncompeting groups in this way. The rate of remuneration would be determined by the demand for those services in relation to the amount of such services available. If they were absolutely noncompeting, the groups would not be affected much by disutility. The intensity of the efforts to get out of a low-paid group and the intensity of the efforts to get into a high remuneration group will be strengthened, if the low-paid group is also a group in which the work is unpleasant and if the high remuneration group is a group in which the work is pleasant. The degree of movement or competition will tend to be made more intense if the gap in attractiveness between them is great. Suppose bricklaying was pleasant and safe and hod carrying was unpleasant and dangerous. As a result of the fact that one was pleasant and safe, hod carriers would try to get into the bricklaying group.

The relative disutility of the occupations in the noncompeting groups might have a little influence on the rates of remuneration within the groups by affecting the amounts of labor offered for hire within each group. The less exacting the work is in a high-paid group, the more hours of labor will that group offer for hire. Assuming a positive supply curve for labor in a low-paid and unpleasant group, unpleasantness will tend to cause the group to offer less hours for hire than if the work were pleasant. There seems to be no doubt that if you want a broad picture of a modern competitive system as it is these days with regard to the relationship between rates of remuneration and the difficulty and unpleasantness of the task, what J. S. Mill said is still true. Remuneration tends to be in inverse proportion to the difficulty and degree of unpleasantness of the task. The hard jobs from the point of view of exertion, fatigue, and strain are the low-paid ones.

The social esteem in which an occupation is held comes somewhat from its remuneration. There may be a vicious circle in an operative sense in that the poorly paid occupations are left to the group that is not able to break its way through into a higher group. Occupations that are poorly paid fall in social esteem so that they become less attractive apart from their rates of remuneration because of the attitude toward them. If you were to look at the occupation of street cleaning as a whole and compare it in usefulness in society with other occupations, we have no precise way of measuring it. The sanitary work of a city is in the higher ranks of usefulness. In the sense of usefulness and honorableness, it ought to be in the highest group. Wages are low, partly because of the ease of the occupation and partly due to the fact that the occupation requires no skill. It is a humble occupation because it is an item of personal service that other persons do not deign to do for themselves. The occupation of the sanitary engineer is dignified enough and is highly paid enough. A certain amount of esteem attaches to it because it is a highly paid task.

Once the rate is low, the occupation loses in social esteem so that there is an additional disutility attached to it.

The thing that ought to attract most attention because it is fundamental to most problems with which the economist concerns himself is the problem of noncompeting groups, the problem of economic inequality.

The problem is more important in the European countries than in the United States, partly because of the extent of the inequality in Europe, and partly because in the United States we are in an earlier stage where we have not achieved all the possibilities of inequality. We are probably moving toward greater inequality.

In this inequality that exists, are the groups noncompeting because of nature or nurture? Are the factors biological or environmental? There has always been some tendency in economic literature to discuss this issue. You may remember that Adam Smith was an equalitarian. From about 1750 to 1820, there was quite a tendency for economists to be equalitarians. Rousseau and William Godwin are examples. In modern times, the genetics school has grown up. This is a technological and biological school. It is their business to find hereditary factors operating, and they work with material where the hereditary factor is most prominent. They jump in their studies from rats and guinea pigs to men and their ways of living. Economics has no contribution to make to this problem, except for the study of observations. Marshall used to make many such observations.

There are great difficulties in the problem, and many of the workers in the field are biased workers. It is almost like the field of government ownership in this respect. Becoming biased is one of the dangers of becoming too engrossed in one's problem. If you want to be an effective propagandist, however, you must become biased.

The problem is to find out what causes these differences. Are they inherent, biological and hereditary, or are they the results of environmental factors? The importance of this question is that if the factors are hereditary, the implication is that it is impossible to do anything about it, and also that it may not be wise to do what you want to do. All that you gain under such circumstances by equalizing is equalizing. If the differences are due to environmental circumstances, then equalizing can mean leveling up, and wise statesmanship may work toward raising a group so that it shall have the capacity to earn wages equal to those of an upper group. If the differences are biological, either you can raise the lower group to the level of the upper group by lowering the upper group or by subsidizing the lower group in some way, giving them extra opportunities so that with that aid they will get on the higher level. In this way, however, the upper group will pay for this, and you will be averaging rather than leveling up.

Galton's work with genius shows that apparently genius is hereditary. A good many of these studies were defective from the scientific point of view.[22]

Karl Pearson began correlating and shows in his series of monographs a high correlation between status and heredity.[23] They showed that in a number of schools in England, children of drunkards did poorly in school. Undernourishment, nervous strain at home, impatience at home, and general mental disorganization of the child in a badly disorganized home might have an effect, however, as well as the hereditary factor. I am not, of course, saying that I know in such a case just how important a part heredity would play. The nature of the problem is such that it has seemed in the past almost impossible to lay out the problem and to get a good scientific test to determine which was the cause and which was the effect.

A new instrument in use is the intelligence quotient. Men have been going into this field from the biological field, and this gives the biological bias. Men sometimes in the educational field have accepted the biological implications. By means of the Alpha tests, intelligence tests, and so on, it has been shown that immigrant stock is inferior in intelligence to native stock and that there has been a deterioration in immigrant stock. The immigrants of thirty years earlier when tested showed higher IQs than the immigrants of ten years ago. The immigrants showed lower IQs than the native population. We are, therefore, lowering the level of our nation by admitting immigration, so it is said. The trouble is that possibly the length of residence in this country has something to do with the return one can make on an IQ test. The fact that the IQ increases with the length of residence in this country would seem to indicate this. A high IQ might mean familiarity with the language.

There are higher IQs in urban districts and lower ones in rural areas. On this basis, you might argue that the urban classes were a selected group. As a theory, you need some evidence, but do not have it.

Work has been done with the Negro in this country in relation to the White. It has been found that the longer southern Negroes have been in a northern town, the higher the IQ, and in schools, the less is the gap between the IQ of the Negroes and that of the Whites. The IQ measures a good deal more than something inherited. The standard intelligence test still measures a large amount of environmental influence.

The 120–140 IQ group is made up almost entirely of those belonging to the highly skilled or professional classes. It is said that the capacity for intellectual growth is inborn in different degrees, that it is hereditary, and that it is closely correlated with social status. On the third point, this is still a completely open question. You might expect some correlation, however.

	Range of IQ	Average IQ
Unskilled labor	63–89	75.5
Semi-skilled labor	74–96	85.2
Skilled labor	84–112	98.3

The study just cited applied only to adults. Turman has succeeded in eliminating the results of the environment.[24] This has not yet been demonstrated. The way to find out would be to consider a sample of 10,000 infants taken at birth and transferred from the North Shore district to the West Side slums and see what they would be forty years later. Turman is now observing foster children. Here in Chicago, they are studying twins separated at birth. IQs differ fairly substantially between the two groups depending on the types of homes they go to.

August 8, 1930

J. B. Clark gets out of his circle by the theory of the simultaneous determination of all the prices of the factors at the same time. There is the framework of the general equilibrium theory; it is a simultaneous determination theory. There is a vicious circle here only if a time lag is introduced, and Clark does not do this. He shows how things happen at the margin.

The zone of indifference is an amateur's crude adaptation of the idea of infinitesimal calculus. This is the only use of the "zone of indifference." Clark uses the term for purposes of explanation or for a display of the forces at work rather than an explanation of how they determine distribution. The contribution of Clark was that he, for the first time in English, presented a theory in which all the factors get their returns determined simultaneously. Interest and wages are residual, and at the same time there is no residual share. There is no order of determination.

This holds true for all prices in a static state. If some factor external to the economy comes into the situation and influences it, then there will not be an order of determination; but it must be remembered that in a static state, everything is at rest and is moving in a static way. There is no friction, and no new factors are coming into the situation. In this universe, all items are mutually determining each other's position. Clark shows this, and this is the heart of his theory. This is his fundamental distinction from the traditional orthodox theory as you find it in J. S. Mill, the Classical School, Taussig, and Walker. It is the only way of solving the problem of the vicious circle.

There is no doubt at all that the business man does not universally operate deliberately and consciously on the basis of marginal productivity theory; and yet if the national income is to be imputed to the various products by natural price processes in accordance with marginal productivity, it must do so because that is the way in which business men are operating. It can do so only to the extent that it is a correct description of the behavior of business men. To a considerable extent, business men operate on a principle that is inconsistent with marginal productivity. It is necessary to operate on the basis of marginal increments of the product and of marginal wages, and accounting is with minor exceptions on the basis of averages, of average costs and prices, and not in terms of marginal increments. The business man is presumably acting in accordance with guidance given him by his accounts. Business men often make the mistake of following the guidance of their accountants. They do not always do so, however, and there is considerable grounds for the belief that on certain questions of policy, the business man, in general, does not see the point of his accountant's advice. The accountant is often wrong, and the business man is right.

There is a transformation going on now in accounting regarding the recognition of the marginal principle. This is the beginning of the development of incremental accounting. In Germany, there is quite a school of accounting that is a marginal school. This school of accounting rests on better economics than the current German economics. In England and this country, the reverse is true.

The business man often recognizes these considerations and follows them in spite of his accountant. The accountant recognizes the differential principle when he recognizes separate accounting for overtime work when there is overtime pay. You will find here and there a special case exposition of incremental cost accounting. This ought to apply through the whole area of business operations except when there is a negative cost curve. Even then you ought to determine the price or output in terms of marginal cost if the company is a quasi-monopoly or in a monopoly position.

The business man may often operate in an unanalyzed fashion and yet conform to the marginal principle. In general, he tends to do so. The use of cost accounting for purposes of guidance in policy is not a matter of very wide extent. Probably a relatively small fraction of American business is based upon any degree of cost analysis. To a large extent, this use is made of cost accounting: The business man finds out what it costs him to produce a certain commodity and he fixes a price and tries to get this price. Cost accounting very often serves to determine what the first price asked shall be, but what the effective price will be is determined by what the business man can get for the output to which he has committed himself.

The relevance to wage theory and collective bargaining is this: that it is a marginal theory that men hire laborers only until their marginal productivity is equal to the wage rate. There is the assertion here that business men operate strictly on the marginal principle. You won't find much evidence that they do so, and you will find appearances that they do not. There are fairly significant divergences from the principle, and many foolish mistakes are made. Many minor divergences are justified by the business man on the ground that computations on minor matters do not pay.

The business man develops a pattern through experience, which tends to avoid those procedures which in the past have worked badly and to maintain those that have worked well. In this way, the type of decision that the business man gives on a cost and price proposition may be one which he cannot explain, but it is based on unanalyzed experience and is likely to be a compromise away from the average cost toward the marginal cost principle. In any case, the correspondence need only be rough for our purposes, provided there is no other pattern that describes the process any more closely. The pattern may be irregular, but you cannot describe the irregularities. All you can do is to describe the extent to which there is a pattern.

There have been attempts to explain wages in terms of relative bargaining power. What does bargaining power consist of and where does labor get its bargaining power? Bargaining power consists of the laborer's marginal productivity. In collective bargaining, there may be holding back for a time with a loss to the employer. If you are assuming full-time working conditions at the time, there is a loss to the employer which is irreparable. The penalty to the employer is the loss of the labor, and the penalty to the laborer is the loss of the wages.

There is this factor of possible idle time through wage difficulties, strikes, lockouts, etc. You may also speak of bargaining power in terms of bargaining skill. This also enters into the situation. We should remember always that the wage contract does not have quantities and that a price without quantities attached to it can be pushed up and down more easily. Except for sunk costs, it would be a matter of little concern to the employer what wages he pays. The lower the wages, the more valuable his investments are. Investment in capital and land is what makes a low wage rate of importance to the entrepreneur. Increasing the wage rate is not nearly so serious for him as it would be if he were not able to vary the amount of labor he uses.

We have a dangerous specialization in American economics. Agricultural economics is interested in presenting a case for the farmer. There are few men who are not pretty frankly advocates rather than scientists. There are certain groups splitting off from the main body of economics.

There is the argument in books on collective bargaining that it can raise the wage rate. Very few economists say that it cannot. There is no theoretical reason why the price of labor cannot be shifted in either direction. The resistance on the part of labor is important, since there is the question of whether it can hold out long enough to force the other side to give way. It is comparatively easy for a labor organization to change the wage rate. It is working with irrational elements and human prejudices, however, and the employers may refuse an increase in the wage rate even though it might have been to their interest to do so. Class prejudice comes in and may make it more difficult to reach a solution.

Thornton gave the following illustration in 1837 to indicate a weakness in the bargaining power of labor.[25] Bargaining between laborers and employers is similar to bargaining between two traders, one of whom is selling oranges and the other who is selling corn. The man selling corn can wait, while the man selling oranges must sell them quickly. In like manner, labor is selling a perishable commodity. The analogy is not altogether happy. Both the employer and the laborer have lost a day if the laborer does not work. They are both in the same position. The loss of time may be more disastrous for the employer than for the employee. The employer has more at stake than does the employee. You can drive a striking employer into bankruptcy, but you drive an employee into starvation, because people will come to his aid before that point is reached. Employers often go bankrupt as the result of a strike.

In some cases, the employer has a peculiarly perishable commodity whose failure to appear on schedule is a great loss to him. Periodical journalism is a good example of this. It is important only if it comes at a specified scheduled time. Almost always a newspaper plant is an organized union plant because of the tremendous hold of the employees on the employers because of this factor. The employer's article has greater perishability. He loses prestige if the periodical does not appear, and lays himself open to suits for failing to fulfill contracts.

Can collective bargaining raise wages without lowering the volume of employment? The general presumption must be in the negative. The qualifications to be made would be somewhat as follows: It is to be understood that the bargaining is to be of the ordinary sort. It can theoretically impose on the employer a higher wage rate if it provides for the volume of employment. In this case, it would be temporary, since the employer would stay in the business only until he had gotten all he could out of his fixed investment. This assumes that the previous situation had been an equilibrium situation. The possibilities of higher wages without a reduction of employment rest on these things happening:

1. The entrepreneur was in error as to the profitable wage for him to pay before.
2. There is the stimulus or the shock argument. The industry may not have been previous to that time as well organized as was reasonable in the light of the circumstances. The increase in wages provided a stimulus of some form to bring about an economy. It might be possible to take care of the costs through a reduction of the technical coefficients of production in one form or another.

Another type of absorption is that in which there was sluggish competition between producers or where there were no diseconomies, the inferior entrepreneurs were not being squeezed out rapidly enough because of a code against price-cutting. Suppose a union forces an increase in wage rates. The more efficient employers can afford to pay this. They do not increase prices, and that forces out some of the inefficient producers and throws their business to the more efficient ones. This lowers technical costs and may also lower technological costs because it means fuller utilization of the plants of the relatively efficient producers. There may be internal economies of scale so that, as the efficient producers get the business of the inferior entrepreneurs, they may expand their plants and get lower real costs as a result. Practically all of these rest on the condition that there was no stable equilibrium beforehand. Inertia elements are important in the description of the actual reality.

August 19, 1930

It is much easier to get a change in wage rates because of the fact that there is no quantity of employment attached to the contract, than it would be if the labor union were bargaining for a wage rate as well as a given volume of employment or sales. The wage rate can move up or down the scale more easily than could a commodity price under collective bargaining. Bargaining power may be used to explain just what wage rate is agreed upon in the conference. The conferees are not bargaining with regard to quantities, and there is no reason why they should hit upon any price or rate except that the lower the rate, the better for the employer and the higher the rate, the more satisfied will be the employees, for the moment at least.

What are the consequences resulting from so-called "collective bargaining" in which a trade union gets a 10 percent increase in wage rates, assuming that under the former wage rate all competent employees had obtained employment. We shall assume that the prevailing previous wage rate was an equilibrium wage rate. Now the rate goes up 10 percent and what happens? The same volume of employment and a higher wage are impossible except on these assumptions:

1. The entrepreneur does not know his business and keeps producing until he goes bankrupt.
2. The employer would have been willing to pay the higher rate before, but there was no competition between the employers for labor. At the rate hitherto prevailing, the employers were looking for more laborers than they were able to get, but they did not raise the price in order to get the volume they wanted.
3. There is the stimulus or shock argument that an increase in wage rates will result in an absorption of the increase in the wage rate in economies. Suppose sluggish competition prevails among the employers and, with an increase in the wage rate, the more efficient employers do not raise their price and the less efficient employers find themselves with an increased money cost. The less efficient employers will now be squeezed out. The more efficient producers can hire all the labor at the higher rate if they take over the plants of those forced out. Fewer competitors may conceivably mean internal economies or the elimination of competitive costs. Trade union leaders have sometimes worked towards the end of eliminating the less efficient entrepreneurs in the industry through raising the wage rate with the understanding

that the more efficient employers would absorb the increase in the wage rate.

There may be a code against price-cutting. Sometimes when employers have a code against frank price-cutting, they are not so careful about concealed price-cutting. The more efficient producers may conceivably absorb the new costs. Complete absorption would take place if the efficient employers gained more by the defeat of their competitors than they lost by the absorption of the costs. The shock of the increased cost may result in tighter management as well as in reduction of waste and economies. This again violates the assumption of the equilibrium situation hitherto prevailing. If the economies were available and possible, then why were they not made before the wage increase? It may take some sort of shock to make an entrepreneur achieve the maximum efficiency of which he is capable. It may act as a stimulus to an invention or to the use of a known technique not previously used. If labor is paid on the time rate, the adjustment may take the form of speeding up the workers so that the wage rate really has not increased. These are the possibilities of absorption.

The following are the possibilities of transfer of the cost to other parties:

1. The shift of the increase of wages may be backward to the persons or interests that sell the entrepreneur the factors he uses. The cost may be shifted to rent, materials, or other laborers. A complete shift without a reduction in volume is not theoretically possible. Shifting can take place only through price changes, and this can take place only through changes in volume. Backward shifting is impossible theoretically without involving some forward shifting.
2. In order to have forward shifting, it is necessary to reduce the volume. Thus, the amounts paid for the factors are reduced and thus you are in a position to reduce the prices you pay for them. This is a new sort of theoretical justification of the approach to the old diffusion theory of taxation. The incidence of taxation must spread itself in various directions. Who bears the brunt of the incidence is a question of the proportions in which the incidence is divided. It depends on the relative elasticities of the landlord's, capitalist's and laborer's demand for the product. It is not to be answered categorically. Forward shifting may be to other labor as consumers, and other labor may, thus, bear the burden. There may be backward shifting through lowering the prices of the things one buys. Except for absorption, therefore, or on account of a previous or subsequent outright error on the part of the entrepreneur, an increase in wages through collective bargaining

always means less employment. In static terms, an increase in wages obtained through collective bargaining, if the previous system was in equilibrium, necessarily causes a reduction in employment unless the stimulus causes an absorption of the new cost.

Whether the loss of labor through less employment is greater or smaller than the increase in wages, whether the aggregate amount paid out as wages increases or decreases, depends on the elasticity of the demand for labor. If the elasticity of the demand for labor were unity, labor in terms of the total size of the wage bill would have nothing to gain from collective bargaining, except on absorption principles. If the elasticity were greater than unity, labor would gain in its total wage bill from collective bargaining. If the labor union gets a 10 percent increase in the wage rate with a 5 percent decrease in employment, and through unemployment funds they take care of the 5 percent unemployed, the union as a whole is better off.

The very low elasticity in the supply of land and capital in the short run tends to make the demand for labor have very low short-run elasticity. This brings about changes unfavorable to successful collective bargaining, if by that one means increases of wage rates plus a minimization of reduction in employment.

In the case of unorganized labor dealing with organized employers or employers who are semi-organized, there is a noncompetitive fixed price to consumers. The upper limit for wages paid will be the marginal productivity of those employed. The maximum limit that the employers would pay would be what the marginal labor which they employ would be worth to them. Presumably the lower limit would be the marginal productivity that the labor would have if all were employed. This might be zero. This is a short-run proposition, and it may be zero even though they were to lower the price of their product. If all labor were employed, the marginal value productivity might still be zero in terms of the demand for that product. The industry may not be equipped efficiently enough to deal with the amount of labor in that occupation. This notion is found in Karl Marx's "reserve army of the unemployed" as a fairly chronic situation. It is probably true that most labor gets more than the marginal labor in that occupation would get if they were all employed.

The marginal productivity is often very low in terms of the existing situation. Theoretically, the most the employer need pay is the marginal productivity if all the labor were employed. Actually, he pays more than that because of both his own morale and the morale of the laborers, as well as the long-run consequences. If he pays lower wages, he may be able to get the labor he wants but the more energetic laborers will try to get out of the industry.

During a period of depression, when all employers and industries were in that situation, any employer knows that if he were to hire all the labor offering itself, the wage he could afford to pay would be very little above zero. At the present time, for instance, at what rate of wages could the steel industry afford to hire all the labor seeking employment in that industry? It probably could not afford to hire them all even at 25¢ per day. If the industry should cut wages in half at present, there is the possibility of a strike. All labor is potentially organized labor and it might revolt en masse. There is also the question of good will and of the moral code to be taken into consideration.

In connection with the theory of the economy of high wages, it is now the business man's philosophy that it pays him to pay high wages. There is a fairly general agreement among business men at the moment that it would not be wise for them to cut wages purely from the point of view of profits. The question is, where does the advantage stop? Where is the gain to the employers? Increasing wages does not increase general purchasing power; it increases only the purchasing power of one group, but some other source will be lowered. You cannot increase something without decreasing something else. This is the point that these theorists overlook. As a continuing thing, there is no sense in the theory at all. There is nothing to be said in defense of it from the business point of view. The entrepreneur, by paying high wages, may be helping the business of someone who manufactures what labor buys, but he may not be helping himself.

It is my opinion that collective bargaining is of much great value to labor when it is with respect to the working conditions rather than with respect to the wage rate. Trade unionism has done little of importance with respect to the wage rate. It is not easy to show for modern countries since 1890 that organized trades have done better than unorganized ones in the matter of wage increases. Here and there, a striking case is found, but here and there also, another striking case is found where a strongly organized craft went to pieces in its economic status under the rule of its trade organization. An industry whose status was almost revolutionized because of skillful collective bargaining is that of the Amalgamated Garment Workers. An example of the other kind that was almost ruined was the soft coal miners. In each case, however, other things enter into the situation. The improvement of working conditions may mean a great deal to the laborers and may mean little to the employer. Concessions can be easily won on this side. On this side, the case for collective bargaining is most obviously to be made, although even here it is extraordinary how little concerned some concerns have been to conditions affecting the comfort and health of the workers.

So far as the bearing on price theory of the questions of trade unionism and collective bargaining is concerned, one simple point to remember is that the theory of collective bargaining is essentially like a theory of taxation, because under taxation also, there is no quantity tied to the price. The government may change the tax without showing much concern as to what happens to quantities. The tax on tobacco may be raised with the expectation that it will not reduce the consumption very much. Legislators do not have any ideas on the subject of the elasticity of demand. They do not foresee the possibilities. The same is true in the case of collective bargaining. The interest is in the price and not in its consequences. No trade union writers discuss these possibilities. If the laborers began fighting for both increased wage rates and the same volume of employment, they then would have a big fight on their hands. Employers, because of their aversion to high wages, may have been paying lower wages than would have been for the maximum advantage to themselves. I am assuming that there is an equilibrium situation to start with.

August 20, 1930

The following is in connection with the solution by von Wieser of the problem of distribution by the use of simultaneous equations[26]:

It is necessary for equilibrium to meet certain stiff conditions in the static state:

1. Each factor should command the same rate in all uses. This is one of the conditions. At the stable equilibrium point, each factor should get the same rate in all occupations.
2. In each industry, the sum total paid to the factors should equal the value of the product. This is a necessary condition of equilibrium.
3. For all industries, all that is produced should be distributed.

We must show that these conditions can continue indefinitely, that the given amount of each factor which is seeking employment at the rate found by the equations will also obtain it, that all the factors which want employment at these rates will get it, and that all employers who want to hire factors at these rates will be able to hire all they want.

The demand for the factor is a marginal productivity function. The amount of each factor that the entrepreneurs will be willing to take at each particular remuneration will be equal to the marginal productivity of that factor. The marginal productivity theory of distribution gets its name not because of its marginal productivity but because marginal productivity was the newest element added.

It is necessary to state the equilibrium in the form of simultaneous equations. All the elements named must be simultaneously determined— prices, marginal productivities, marginal and demand and supply prices, coefficients of production, and marginal utilities—unless they were given originally. Coefficients of production are not fixed.

Interest

Irving Fisher's new version of his *Rate of Interest* called *The Theory of Interest* has recently been published.[27] His book gives as near to a definitive statement of the theory of interest as we have today. There are some things included that I think ought to be left out, but they are not connected with the mechanical aspects of the situation. *The Rate of Interest* was an attack on the productivity theory of interest. His new book is a statement of the productivity theory, and Fisher now denies that he ever attacked the productivity theory. Fisher and Fetter were two opponents of the productivity theory. Fisher has now gone over to the other camp and that leaves Fetter alone.

In order to follow J. B. Clark's theory of interest, one must bear in mind his distinction between capital and capital goods.[28] Capital goods must be destroyed if capital is to be perpetuated. Capital has complete mobility, and capital goods have almost no mobility. Capital is a fund of value actually embodied in concrete capital goods. It is the capitalization aspect of capital goods.

What is to be said about intangible capital, such as patent rights, goodwill, and franchises, etc.? Trade names are held and valued at certain amounts and can be sold separately, and yet they are not concrete goods. It is possible to sell a mailing list. Is that a concrete capital good? How about "sucker" lists? Are they concrete capital goods? Goodwill has been a legal and a property category from at least the fourteenth or the fifteenth century, at least in Switzerland. This difficulty may be met by saying that capital goods are not always concrete and material. Capital goods may be both tangible and intangible. Land, Clark says, is the only permanent capital good. Capital is permanent. This is true only under the assumption of his static state in which there are no catastrophes and no bankruptcies. As one reads on in Clark, he forgets the emphasis on the static state and seems to feel that Clark has forgotten it too. There is a widespread belief that capital itself is not very permanent, because it tends to be wasted.

Rent is the aggregate of the lump sums earned by capital goods, whereas interest is the fraction of itself earned by the permanent fund of capital. Interest is a fraction of itself that is earned by the permanent fund of capital; this statement is all right. Proximately, Clark says, rent fixes interest. Fundamentally, interest governs rents. By this, he means that if a given capital good yields, say, a product to the value of $5.00 a year, then that is the rent it yields. If you want to find the rate of interest, then find out what percentage to the capital $5.00 is, and that is the rate of interest. By this, he means that capital will be put into such forms as will equalize its returns in all uses.

The central problem of interest is what determines the physical productivity of capital and what is the relationship between the physical productivity of capital and a rate percent quoted on the market.

The most characteristic phase of interest theory is that only the creation of capital goods calls for abstinence. In the static state, no abstinence is required. He says that abstinence is confined to the genesis of new capital. This is a good example of the use of the word "virtually." His statements are not true, since capital accumulation does require abstinence. Clark uses the example of a forest that, he says, maintains itself after it is once planted. Is taking the mature timber as it grows all you can do with a fifty-year-old forest? It is possible to use immature timber, and the community may do this.

It is possible to hasten the rate of using up of any kind of capital good by reducing the maintenance fund, and the spendthrift does this. In an examination of Cassel on this point, you would find that he was never able to make up his mind. It is possible, perhaps, to make a differentiation between an initial decision to do something and to continue doing what you had originally decided to do.

In periodicals and elementary textbooks, you find quite a few writers who have been influenced by Clark's exposition and have not seen that it does not hold. The only explanation of how Clark came to state this proposition is the notion of the perpetual duration of capital, capital goods having been fixed in form so that they shall wear out at a certain pace. In order that they endure perpetually, it is necessary to provide a replacement fund. This requires decision and willpower. If you do not provide for a replacement fund, your capital will disappear with the capital goods. The rate at which the capital goods disappear is limited by the technological character of the capital goods. In any form of capital, you can think of some decision to abstain from immediate consumption, which is necessary in order that the manifestation of it shall continue. Without this notion, ordinary abstinence has no meaning at all.

In the case of the forest taking fifty years to ripen and then becoming self-maintaining, if there is no possible advantage that you can gain from cutting down the forest, so far as the community is concerned, they are committed to that amount of saving and it does not require any further abstinence. Such cases, however, are rare. As between individuals, it is possible to make the forced maintenance of that amount of capital act as a substitute for the creation of new capital which otherwise would have been created. Even there, therefore, willpower is necessary. If interest is not a return for abstinence, what is the ethical basis for the payment of interest? The economic basis is that capital is productive.

Clark says: "It is of the nature of the bow to add something to the hunter's product."[29] That is another statement having a sixteenth-century flavor. You would be hard pressed to find in economic literature of the twentieth century many passages of that particular flavor.

August 21, 1930

Clark gives a diagram like this one to support his point that there is no difference in the relationship to price, of interest as a cost, or land rent as a cost, or wages as a cost, and he says that the traditional Ricardian way of showing that rent does not enter into the cost which determines price can be applied to any other of these factors. In this diagram, there is a given amount of labor applied in successive units to a given amount of capital. The first unit of labor would produce *BA* until all the labor is used, and the last unit would produce *CD*. Multiply this by the number of units of labor, and all of the rectangle *AECD* goes to wages. The rate times the number of units of labor gives the total payroll.

If interest as a rate is wanted, reverse the process and take the same amount of labor and apply to the units of labor successive units of capital.

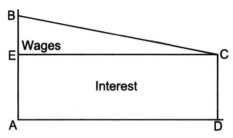

Labor will get the sum of the differences between the yield of the early units of capital and the yield of the marginal unit. The wages area will be equal to the interest area in the previous diagram. Every factor can be regarded as obtaining its income as the sum of the differentials between what the first units yield and what the marginal units yield when applied to the equilibrium amount of the new factors.

If, in the first diagram, only *AF* units of labor were applied to a given amount of capital, the marginal productivity of labor would have been *HF* and the capital would have obtained in interest only the triangle *BGH*. If the total amount of interest is smaller, obviously the rate must be smaller.

The above two diagrams have had as much influence as anything Clark has written, and the ideas in them are to be found repeated in the literature. He is trying to show either the reduction of Ricardian rent theory to an absurdity by showing that by the same process of reasoning, every distributive share becomes a differential from a zero margin, or else, it is a generalization of the Ricardian concept showing that it does really apply. I am not sure which of these ideas is in Clark's mind, but I think that the latter is the case, showing that it is true for all the factors. It seems fairly clear that most of the people who have been influenced have interpreted it as a generalization of the Ricardian rent theory rather than making it ridiculous for any one factor.

Is there anything to be said against this theory? What answer would Ricardo have made to it? The question now is whether interest gets determined in the same way that rent gets determined or in the same way that wages get determined. Is it possible to show that interest is a differential in the way in which rent is a differential? Let me first point out that the

Ricardian rent differential is of two forms, one of which he emphasizes, but the other one of which is more important. In rent theory, we go ahead without bothering to discuss the difference in the rate of income to different pieces of land. We do not make our factors homogeneous, and we discuss the differences in rent which different pieces of land yield; whereas for capital, practically invariably, and for labor generally, we assume homogeneity of the factors.

Suppose you are dealing with differences in wages to different persons. That is closer to the ordinary discussion of rent theory than is the discussion of wages in terms of a uniform kind of homogeneous labor. Ricardo also used this kind of a differential, whereas you can imagine that he was thinking in terms of homogeneous land units. He always took the land as the thing to which the other factors were being applied. Clark is applying successive doses of factor *A* to factor *B*. Ricardo never applies successive doses of land to labor. He applies successive doses of labor to land or from land, but he never reverses the process.

Ricardo would have said that in the circumstances assumed by Clark, he puts deliberately all the factors into the same situation. He says nothing about one factor which is not true about another, except one thing he says about capital, namely, that it maintains itself without requiring abstinence.

Is Clark dealing with a supply of labor that is variable depending on its rate of remuneration? Here, Clark is assuming not merely a static state, but also one in which there is a given amount of the factors which must be used. He is assuming a static state with an equilibrium condition in which all the factors are employed to the full. Clark assumes that there is so much of the factors, all of them at work, and that they will accept whatever marginal rate they have to when they are in that situation. The Ricardian rent theory is based on the assumption that the situation is thus for land but not for any other factor. This is a generalization of the Ricardian rent theory which Ricardo would have accepted if he had accepted the assumptions, namely that the factors are given in amount and that they have no reservation prices. Ricardo's rent theory is based on the doctrine that land has no reservation price, whereas capital and land have. The landlord will take for his rent whatever he can get if he cannot get something more. This labor will not do. In the long run, there is another alternative, the possibility of less labor through influence on the population. Capital also will not accept whatever rate it happens to be able to earn; if the rate is not high enough to satisfy the capitalists, they will convert the capital to consumption purposes.

The basic function is that land as a supply condition is different from the supply condition of the other factors. This discussion leaves Ricardian theory intact in terms of Ricardian assumptions, but it is perfectly all right in terms of Clarkian assumptions.

When two able men disagree, you will very often find that they are starting out with something different in assumptions that were unobserved at the start. The difference in assumptions is obviously a question of fact. Actually, information of an informative sort is extremely difficult to get on this particular issue. You will find that the able economists who accept Clark's proposition do so on the grounds that there is no significant difference in the nature of the supply functions for land and the supply functions for other factors.

One or two economists have reversed the proposition by saying that the supply functions of land are the same as the functions of labor and capital, that the amount of labor is given by the amount of population, and that the amount of capital at any one time is a given and saving is determined to only an insignificant extent by the rate of interest. This assumes that the motives to saving are other things than the interest income.

Given the labor and capital as independent of the rates of remuneration, they then proceed to argue that the amount of land can be increased. They give the impression that the amount of land gets to be highly variable as the rate of remuneration changes, and that it is the only factor which is variable. The facts are more as Ricardo stated them than as the modern critics have it.

I think that I have succeeded very well in this quarter in keeping any information out of this course. We are interested in the tools of analysis and of thought and not in reaching positive conclusions. In any case, I am not sure that I would know how to get information supporting my belief. It might be possible, but it would be a very difficult task. We are speaking now of the factors at large, not of the factors entering into the production of any particular commodity.

Let us return to Clark's argument that no abstinence is required to maintain capital, but that abstinence is required only at the genesis of new capital. For a static state, the rate of interest must equal the marginal value productivity of capital. If the rate of interest were high, entrepreneurs would not be willing to hire all capital available for hire. If the marginal productivity of capital were higher than the going rate of interest, entrepreneurs would bid competitively for the hire of the available capital and would bid up the rate until only at a rate of interest equal to marginal productivity would there be equilibrium. Marginal value productivity would equal the rate of remuneration. One must remember that a static state is one in which the factors will arrange themselves in a certain grouping, and such a rate will not be disturbed unless some extraneous factor comes in. It is not possible to show that, if there is no abstinence, no irksomeness connected with waiting and with the maintenance of capital, the amount of capital would remain unaltered in that state.

Let us suppose, at the margin:
$100 income = 1,000 utils of present consumption, 1929 (1,000)
$100 income = 1,000 utils present valuation of 1930 consumption (950)

This is a non-equilibrium situation, so long as interest is being paid. If you get 5 percent per year on income which you convert into capital and do not consume now, it is a mistake for you to take $100 now. You are losing $5.00 at the margin instead of investing it. Part of one's income would be invested by the rational individual until he decreases his monetary present income, and he increases his prospective future income and decreases the present valuation of its marginal utility, and brings the two into such a relationship that the present value of $100 shall be to the present value of $100 next year $= \frac{1}{1-i}$.

$$\frac{1}{1-i} = \frac{\text{present value of } \$100 \text{ now}}{\text{present value of } \$100 \text{ next year}}$$

or

$$\frac{1}{1 - \text{marginal product per year}} = \frac{\text{present value of } \$100 \text{ now}}{\text{present value of } \$100 \text{ next year}}$$

or

Marginal value product per year = Marginal time preference per year

These must be equal in order to have equilibrium. In Clark's system, if he means by the non-necessity of abstinence, by the argument that capital maintains itself, that there will be no time preference in the static state, then he has a noncompetitive situation. It is impossible to have a marginal net productivity without having a marginal time preference in favor of the present. If he has a marginal time preference, then he is exercising what the old economists meant by abstinence. If one takes both the interest and waiting together, then one has no net abstinence. The abstinence has been rewarded. If one takes the labor and the wages paid for the labor together, there is no net disutility.

You have not disposed of abstinence as a cost unless once you have made the decision to save it and it becomes physically impossible to cut down on the amount of the capital. Clark could have made an assumption approaching this situation if he had assumed that all capital in the static state had been acquired by inheritance, and by trust deeds which gave the beneficiaries access merely to the income, but would not enable them to get at the capital. In that case, the capital, if reasonably well managed, would have maintained itself without a decision necessary on the part of any individual. Under such circumstances, you are artificially tying up the use that can be made of wealth. Under those circumstances, you would have Clark's situation. In that case, you could have equilibrium, but you would have it because men would not be able to decide on the basis of these equalities.

Suppose that an estate yielded only 2 percent per year and the beneficiary had a time preference of 15 percent per year. There is nothing he could do about it. The estate would be tied up and he could not get at it. The will to save was not being exercised by him or anyone else, and the capital was being maintained through the law by the will of a person who was dead.

This would be a non-equilibrium situation on the basis of a rational individualistic society. Individual A who was dead at that time could control individual B's behavior. Even then, it would be consistent with Clark's conclusions only in one direction. Suppose that the capital were actually producing 10 percent per year and the marginal time preference per year was 5 percent. There would be nothing in the trust deed to prevent the beneficiaries from saving out of their income under these circumstances, and the amount of capital would increase until the marginal productivity were brought down until it equaled the time preference.

With trust limitations, it is conceivable that marginal time preference could exceed marginal value productivity, but it is not conceivable how marginal productivity could exceed time preference for any period of time. If it did, the people would do saving for themselves. That would increase the amount of capital and would lower the marginal productivity of capital, and increase the time preference. It is only in one direction, even with the trust deed, that it is possible to have equilibrium even though marginal productivity was not equal to marginal time preference.

It is conceivable to imagine a society in which inaccessibility of the estates for immediate consumption might become a social institution that must not be violated. Each individual would like to get at the money, but each individual would share in the social sense that it is a sin to do that. In any case, for our theoretical purposes, I want to point out the implications in Clark's theory. It is novel because he introduces striking and strange assumptions. In the case of the maintenance of capital, there is no evidence supporting him.

Let us return to his point that it is of the nature of the bow to add enough to the product to enable the hunter to make another one when the old one has worn out. Is it in the nature of a bow to do this? Böhm-Bawerk asserted this for a time and then conceded that it was not so.[30] The question depends on the number of bows the hunter already has. The laborer can produce more than he can without it, but there is not necessarily net productivity unless the bow adds to what the hunter catches more than could have been caught in the time necessary to make the bow. The net productivity of capital is the product in excess of what is necessary to repay those who made the capital. Even if one argues that the hunter can catch more, it does not follow that the capital good adds sufficient to the product to more than replace itself. Most capital yields an interest.

Clark would make it as part of the nature of capital. What makes capital yield a net interest? What other explanation is there for the fact that it is not the nature of capital to yield a net interest? The only explanation which Clark offers is that it is in the nature of the bow to produce more than is sufficient to replace itself.

August 22, 1930

I shall have to confine myself to that problem which has been most controversial, the relation between physical productivity and a percent rate of interest.

Böhm-Bawerk denied the productivity theory of interest, but he argued that one of the factors determining interest, and which by itself would be sufficient to produce interest, was the technical superiority of present over future goods.[31] By productivity, Böhm-Bawerk meant productivity in some metaphysical sense, a distinct separate productivity in the sense of creative responsibility. Technical superiority is the increase in output which results from lengthening the production period by one unit of time, other things remaining the same. Böhm-Bawerk is showing the marginal productivity of waiting. He does not handle the differential concept at all well, but the first column in his tables is the marginal productivity of waiting when applied to given amounts of land and labor. Böhm-Bawerk argues that you can have interest with technical superiority, even though you do not have the other two factors, relative provision for the future and discount of the future, what he calls "underestimate of the future." In the underestimate of the future, he includes a number of items, not all of which are underestimate. The uncertainty of life is not an underestimate. Some are prudential items. You do not know how long you are going to live and you consume now because you may not be here next year. This would be a rational adjustment; it would not be an underestimate.

This underestimate of the future is an error element that forms a part of the regular economic system of most of the classical and neoclassical economists. It is a departure from the assumption of the intelligent, rational economic man. Part of the classical and neoclassical system is the concept of a man who follows his interests rationally except with respect to perspective as to time. Here they introduce an error element and see a general bias so that they can use it as a general premise and reason from it.

It has been shown by critics of Böhm-Bawerk, especially by a statistician in the University of Berlin, that Böhm-Bawerk is wrong in saying that technical superiority alone would produce interest. If he does not underestimate the future, technical superiority would not lead to interest. Fisher also demonstrates this adequately.

Böhm-Bawerk had said that technical superiority could stand alone and proves that he can take out each one of the other two factors at a time and show that there would still be interest. However, when he discusses taking both other factors at the same time, he says that that would lead to an absurd basis, because without either of the other factors, production periods would be infinitely long, because that is how output is maximized. If the individual would wait until infinity, that would create a difference in relative provision. There would be no present goods and there would be a large amount of future goods. Present goods would rise and there would be developed a discount of the future. Here he is saying, in fact, that it is impossible to have a technical superiority existing without the contemporary existence of a time preference, not that you can have interest without a discount of the future, as he had argued.

Critics make too much of this flaw in Böhm-Bawerk's reasoning. His technical superiority has been accepted by everybody since his time as being essentially the productivity notion of other economists. He was wrong in insisting that technical superiority alone could result in the existence of an interest rate.

The impression that Fisher gives and has given to two decades of students is that as a result of Böhm-Bawerk's one failure, his whole theory breaks down. If you were to change the technical superiority in any way, Böhm-Bawerk would show that interest was a function of technical superiority and also a function of other things. Any change in technical superiority will operate to change the rate of interest. That is the essential contribution of Böhm-Bawerk's tables. Fisher overlooks this and shows that Böhm-Bawerk's statement was bad with respect to one point that is of no special significance. We do have an underestimate of the future and a difference in relative provision. Since we can never have one of these alone, what does it matter whether or not we could have interest if one were alone?

Böhm-Bawerk's tables show that the rate of interest is affected by any change in relative provision, technical superiority, or rate of change in discount of the future.

Any comments I make on Fisher dealing with productivity are in reference to his original book.

We will take up two of Fisher's illustrations: his orchard case and his machine case, as attempts to show the fallacy of the productivity theory. A ten-acre orchard yields one hundred barrels per year that sell for $1,000. The orchard is worth $20,000. The rate of interest is, therefore, 5 percent. How shall we relate this to the productivity of capital? You cannot say that the orchard yields 1/5 of itself because it yields apples. How can you figure apples as a percentage of trees? It is not because the orchard is worth $20,000 that the annual crop will be worth $1,000. The interest rate is not 5 percent because the $20,000 orchard yields a $1,000 crop per year. The orchard is worth $20,000 because it yields $1,000 per year and the interest rate is 5 percent.

The fact that capital goods get their capital value as a capitalization of their yield at the current rate of interest is overlooked. The orchard is a $20,000 orchard only because it yields $1,000 a year and the interest rate happens to be 5 percent.

Let us say that it is an important industry and the interest rate is 5 percent. There is an opportunity to use capital at an extraordinary profit, say of 20 percent. The entrepreneur would go about trying to borrow capital in order to put it into the building of orchards. The adjustment will not be merely increased output of fruit and, therefore, a fall in the interest yield of the capital goods, but there also will be a rise in the interest rate and a rise in land rents and wages. The rush to make orchards will raise the value of land and raise wages so that the adjustment will not be merely an adjustment in the value of the orchard. The whole equilibrium situation will change, and in the new situation every price will be different. All that Fisher did is to lay down as a necessary condition of equilibrium that the value of a capital good must equal its annual yield capitalized at the current rate of interest. In the case of land having no cost of production, its value is a capitalization of its productivity.

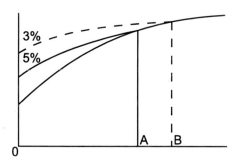

Suppose the market rate of interest is 5 percent. Draw a line representing the interest at 5 percent, which will be tangent to this curve. *OA* is the proper length of time that the trees should be allowed to grow. It is true that the physical rate of growth here coincides with the interest rate, which is what the productivity theorist has claimed. In this case, Fisher says, this proposition can be laid down. There is a physical rate of growth that is comparable to the market rate of interest. The point at which it is economical to stop is determined by the market rate of interest instead of determining the market rate of interest. You have the 5 percent market rate, and this determines what the cutting rate shall be.

Thomas Manley lays down the doctrine that the rate at which a forest should be cut should be determined by the interest rate and should be such that the rate of growth is equal to the rate of interest. He laid down this doctrine in 1663 in his *Interest of Money Examined*.[32] It is quite possible that practical foresters have seen this since time immemorial. What is the bearing on the doctrine that either you cannot get a physical rate of productivity comparable to the interest rate or that there is a range of physical productivity and the interest rate selects which one shall be the actual rate to be followed?

Suppose the rate of interest falls to 3 percent. The cutting rate is indicated on the above chart. The trees will then stand for forty years instead of thirty years, and the proper length of time for the trees to grow will be *OB*. On this basis, men will begin to borrow in order to increase the range of their forests. They will want to borrow also because they will not be getting cash. They will borrow to continue the growth over the longer period. In the meantime, there will be a reduction in the rate of cutting, which will raise the price of timber. There will be two causal factors: a reduction in the demand for labor for cutting timber and an increase in the demand for labor for starting new forests. Under these circumstances, there will be an increase in the demand for capital at 3 percent, and also the value of the product will fall. There will be a new equilibrium situation. The entrepreneurs can probably get all the capital they want at 3 percent. The necessity that the rate of interest equals the physical rate of production is not a necessity merely that you follow that rate of production which equals the rate of interest, but that whichever rate of production you choose (whichever amount of capital you use) will affect the demand for capital and, therefore, will have its effect on the interest rate.

Suppose that a new invention is able to shorten the period to maturity of trees by ten years. Suppose that before this that 5 percent was an equilibrium rate. If the price were as it is now and instead of having to wait forty years, it is necessary to wait only thirty years, the forests become a more attractive investment and there would be a rush into this industry. The rush into this industry would raise the rate of interest and increase the borrowing of capital. In time, also, it would lower the value of timber, with more timber being produced. The rate of growth would be changed.

If the rate of interest changed to 6 percent, then it would pay to cut sooner and the cost of production of a forest would equal its value based on its annual yield capitalized at the market rate of interest. If there is no cost of production, it is not freely reproducible. It is either a free good or is limited by nature, and that sets what its physical rate of productivity will be.

Supposing that you have this situation: a natural orchard or a natural forest, growing at the rate of 5 percent a year, and a free good. How would you reconcile the rate of 5 percent in physical growth with the interest? If the capital good is a free good, then its crop will be free. If its crop has net value, a value over the cost of gathering it, then the thing that produces it will have value. This is a sticker for the productivity theorist. There is a high rate of physical productivity and yet there is no interest. The answer is that it has to produce valuable goods in order that there shall be an interest problem.

Fisher also gives the case of a machine with ten years of life, which produces services worth $100 annually. The interest rate is 5 percent. The value of the machine is worth $772. Suppose the services of the machine double in quantity. A unit of service will not remain the same in price if you double its output. Fisher implies that the services may be worth $200 per year under these conditions. I think that he means more than $100 per year. The value of the machine would go down somewhat in terms of units of service, but the new value will be more than $100. Whatever the effect on income, the capital value will change so as to approximate the new income capitalized at the current rate of interest. He is suggesting that there may be some effect on the rate of interest in a change in productivity. One might say that the rate of interest varies with the marginal value productivity, but it is better to say that one of the conditions of equilibrium is that the rate of interest is equal to the rate of marginal value productivity. It is not a good way of stating a proposition to say that marginal anything determines anything else. Where the margin shall be is one phase of the general determination.

What does an economist mean when he says that the productivity is doubled? An economist is legitimately interested in either the physical phase or the value phase. For purposes of equilibrium, the equilibrium must be between the value productivity and the market rate of interest, but unless you assume changing value, a definite trend per unit of value, the rate of physical productivity, and the rate of value productivity must coincide when compared on the same basis. The rate of productivity is the rate of output as a percentage of the preceding output resulting from an increase of one unit in the amount of waiting, other things remaining the same. The marginal rate of productivity is the increase in percent in output from using a period of waiting $x + 1$ as compared with using a period of waiting x. That rate need not necessarily be the value rate. If in the time interval you can count on a fall of say, 50 percent in the value of a product each year, the physical rate or productivity will be 10 percent roughly, and the value rate of productivity will be 5 percent.

An economist who says that price varies with demand does not say that a doubling of demand doubles price; therefore, by doubling the productivity, it is not known what the effect will be on the rate of interest. All that it is possible to say about the interest rate is that it will rise, other things remaining the same. No productivity theorist would say that it would double.

Fisher was right so far as he went but he did not go far enough. He was showing that productivity alone would not determine interest, but that there were other factors involved. Nobody ever denied this. He did not show that productivity was a passive element and that the situation had to adjust itself to the prevailing rate of interest. Economists were not convinced by Irving Fisher's statements, although you do in the literature run across references to Fisher's successful demonstrations.

There is a great deal more on the theory of interest that I wish I had time to expound. There has been a lot of discussion in recent years as to the nature of the supply curve of capital. Cassel's theory is simple and plausible, apparently, that the probable duration of life is the important factor, but it does not stand up either a priori or inductively, because the savings curves for individuals do not seem to go in the direction he indicates. Some years earlier, Mixter wrote on the question of the saver's surplus, and said that the rate of interest would equal the rate of marginal time preference only at the margin.[33] If the savings curve, the abstinence curve, the irksomeness of waiting or saving increased, as you increase the percentage of each year's income that you were setting aside for saving, and that, therefore, there would be that equilibrium at the margin between the utility of the rate of interest and the disutility of the savings, then you would have a surplus on all the other units. This is just like the worker's surplus. At the margin, presumably, there is a balance between what he gets from his last unit of labor and the pain of doing it. On the earlier units there is a surplus.

It has been argued that most of saving is painless, and stress has been placed on corporate saving. There is no doubt that it can be shown that a large part of the saving is done by corporations through the plowing back of their earnings rather than distributing them to shareholders. A decision has to be made, but the decision is made for the individual. He can, however, escape from it. So far as national or community saving is concerned, if Jones desires to spend his savings, he can spend them whether the corporation distributes them or not; Jones can spend them through cooperation with Smith whereby Smith takes over this sort of saving and Smith would not have to have some other form of saving created for him.

August 25, 1930

Let x = ultimate physical productivity of one unit of labor devoted to making capital goods where fruition in consumable goods takes time t.

Let y = present physical productivity of one unit of labor devoted to making immediately consumable goods.

Assume that the prices of the products are constant through time. Let i = rate of interest.

Then, $\dfrac{x-y}{ty}$. This is on the assumption of simple interest.

$(1+i)^t = \dfrac{x}{y}$. This is the compound interest formula.

Suppose that $x = 1,100$ units of product in two years and that $y = 1,000$ units immediately. Let us assume that the marginal productivity of the plows which a man can make in one year is 1,100 units of wheat, but it is available two years after the beginning of the work in making the plows. The laborer using the plows produces 1,000 bushels immediately. Suppose that the rate of interest is 5 percent. A plow would be worth fifty bushels a year, and the depreciation would be 50 percent per year. The plow would produce 550 bushels a year for two years. The plow would then be worth something under 1,100 bushels. This is in accordance with Fisher's original formula in which he is trying to throw out productivity.

Suppose there is a sudden decrease in the physical productivity of capital so that x drops to 1,050 units and y drops to 1,000 units.

$$\text{The interest} = \frac{1050 - 1000}{2000} = 2\frac{1}{2}\%.$$

Now the plow yields 2½ percent, whereas the return of interest is 5 percent per year. By decreasing one factor, leaving the other factor constant, and increasing the marginal productivity of the factor you have decreased, you increase the productivity of the marginal factors.

Suppose that x rises to 1,060 and y falls to 980.

$$\frac{1060 - 980}{980 \times 2} = \frac{80}{1760} = 4.4\%.$$

The demand for capital in this industry has fallen off. With the falling off in the demand for capital, 4.4 percent might become the market rate of interest. Wages would have fallen because of the decreased productivity and decreased demand for labor in terms of what they are willing to pay in the industry. In every case, you would have to pay for plows what their labor costs, and their price would be their cost of production or the discounted value of their yield during their useful life. These two things would have to equilibrate. Here you have the productivity determining the rate of interest, although given the rate of interest, that rate of interest will determine what types of combinations shall be used between the products. It is a mutual reaction, and the equilibrium requires that the value of a capital good equal its cost of production and that it also equal the discounted capitalization or the discounted value of the series of net yields that it will make during its useful life.

If the price according to the cost of production were higher than the discounted capitalization of the net yields, then it would be an unprofitable sort of capital good to manufacture. Reducing its output would increase its marginal physical product, and thus its marginal value product, and, therefore, would presumably have lowered its cost of production; these two would, therefore, come into equilibrium. There would have to be adjustments from the point of view of the productivity of labor such that the physical productivity of the capital will equal the market rate of interest.

If you assume that the prices of the products change through time, if you assume beforehand that there will be certain anticipated changes in the price of the products, then the lower rate of interest cannot be equal to the physical rate of marginal productivity of capital, because you have to modify that physical rate by the differences in the value of that product according to whether it comes this year or next; if the physical marginal productivity of capital were 5 percent and each year the price of the product sank 5 percent, the net yield of the capital would be zero in value. Each year, there would be five more units than before, but they would be worth 5 percent per unit less than before, and there would be no return on the investment. This is the phenomenon which Irving Fisher thought he discovered, that you have to take into account the difference in the value from one year to the next in order to get the true interest. This is not a discounting of the future, but rather a comparison of the values of particular units as they were determined in the 1920s and 1930s. This has to be adjusted in order to get the real rate of interest. It is Fisher's real rate of interest which ought to be equal to the physical rate of the marginal productivity of capital.

Fisher emphasizes the differences in the purchasing power of money. Let us assume that the price of a particular commodity relative to other prices is going to go down by 5 percent per year. Then, there would have to be a 10 percent increase in productivity in order to get a 5 percent increase in yield. Fisher says that it is necessary to get a 10 percent rate per year in normal rate if the price is rising by 5 percent per year in order to get a real yield of 5 percent per year on the original investment. At one time, Fisher presented as the main explanation of business cycles these divergences between real interest and nominal interest. You will find in his *Rate of Interest* an attempt at an inductive demonstration that men operate on this basis and then when prices are rising, interest rates rise and vice versa because when men see that when prices are rising, they need to get a higher market rate of interest to get a true rate of interest. I do not think that this is a valid explanation. During a period of rapidly depreciating currency, the high interest rate may be a means of protection against depreciated money in which repayment is going to be made.

There is a positive correlation between the price level and the rate of interest, but there is a better explanation than this. Rising prices are periods of business expansion either because prices expand when business expands or because price expansion itself is a stimulus to business. In any case, upward swings of the business cycle have been accompanied by upward movements of the price level. These are periods in which entrepreneurs think that they can do much with their capital, and, therefore, they borrow capital. The demand for capital has a cyclical fluctuation that corresponds somewhat to the business cycle.

In Fisher's new terminology, the cycle would be a result of the realization of opportunity for investment. Let us call it "anticipated productivity" or "higher anticipations of productivity." This explains the cycle of the interest rate more than a cycle of deviations between the market rate and the true interest rate because of a decline in the purchasing power of money.

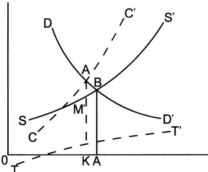

We have in the above diagram from Carver the supply and demand curves for goods based on their cost of production.[34] *T-T'* is the time preference curve resulting from men's aversion beyond a certain point to wait for the return of their income for their effort. It is found necessary to modify the supply curve for the influence of the time preference, so that the capital good shall have to more than replace itself. If it only replaced itself, only the principal would be gotten back; an interest return would be lacking. Carver argues that the supply curve is, thus, modified.

When a producer of goods sells them, he gets KL and the cost of production will be KM exclusive of ML, which will be the return for the waiting that has been done. The effect of this time preference will be to restrict the supply of capital goods until their value is based on marginal product.

Fisher stresses the equalization of income through time, with the evening of income serving as a factor in saving or borrowing, and states that men borrow in order to equalize their income stream now as compared with their stream in the future. They save because they anticipate smaller incomes in the future. As a matter of fact, this is a very minor factor. Men do not think about the timing of their income. If they are wealthy, then problems of equalization cease to be existent. If they are very poor, they will be more inclined to borrow and then, perhaps, Fisher's statement is a factor, but this is not a significant factor in the community. Fisher attempts to show that business men borrow on a personal income equalization principle. Obviously, this principle ought not to apply to corporate borrowings. For the individual businessman, if he has $10,000 and borrows $100,000 more, he does so because he thinks that he can make money with the borrowed money. If the profits come the year during which the money is borrowed, it would be worth 5 percent more to him than if the profits came the next year. The business man wants to make money, and the timing is a negative factor in the situation. In his *L'Interet du Capital*, Landry brought out this situation, but Irving Fisher has made much more of it.[35]

There has been some suggestion that there is a positive demand curve for capital. This results from the same factor that led Henry Moore to think of a positive demand schedule for iron.[36] Expansion periods are periods of heavy construction activities and, therefore, have increased demands for pig iron; expansion periods are also periods of high prices. What you have here is the coincidence that the years of high demand shall also be years of high prices. In the years of business optimism, there is the expectation that men will be willing to make large investments and to pay high rates; whereas in the years of depression, even at a low rate, small amounts of capital will be borrowed. It is not necessary to assume the positive slope of the demand curve.

There is the proposition for distribution theory that the demands for the generalized non-specialized factors of production are highly elastic. The entrepreneur wants factors because of what they will add to the product.

There are no great peculiarities in the demands for the particular factors unless these factors are specialized, and, therefore, any peculiarities in them will be reflected. There is great elasticity in the demand for any one factor largely because so much substitution is possible between the factors, Taussig's fixed state of the arts to the contrary notwithstanding.

This is a great difficulty in the marginal productivity theory and is one that has not yet been faced. Marginal productivity theory rests on the assumptions that the factors are complementary and the universal law of diminishing returns is based on this assumption, but the factors may be rival more than they are complementary under certain circumstances.

Cannan makes something of the argument that a sudden doubling of the productivity of capital might reduce the per-capita income of labor.[37] It is usually reasonable to accept the universal law of diminishing returns and assume that the factors are complementary and that an increase of one means an increased remuneration for all the others.

In his article on "Saver's Surplus and the Interest Rate" in the *Quarterly Journal of Economics* in 1921, Wolf accepts the Anderson theory that banks can increase capital through bank credit.[38] What banks do is to increase the extent to which existing capital is being utilized. In addition, by stimulating business and income, they may stimulate new saving and, thus, lead to the existence next year of more capital than if the banks had not extended credit. However, banks cannot add directly to the existing amount of capital simply by extending loans on their books.

It is possible to make a distinction between creating capital and stimulating an increased use of the existing amount of capital and bringing into existence forces that will create capital in the future as a result of certain actions.

A bank creates capital only in the way in which an orator creates warriors. The orator makes men willing to be soldiers. On that basis, Wolf is trying to find out whether the creation of capital needs abstinence. The point is that the bank does not do the saving. When a bank lends $10,000, it does not create $10,000 more capital than before. The loan is not made by the bank; the loan is made by the persons who accept your checks on the bank as payment for capital goods. You may get $9,500 and buy machines with this. The man who sold you the machines may deposit this in the same bank from which you borrowed it and leave it there. The bank has certificated your credit. The man who accepts your check is actually the lender of the capital goods. The bank lends you a certification of your credit for three months that you are good for $9,500.

The man who sold you the machinery may deposit your check and draw on the deposit and buy from somebody else. He has kept it for two days and for those two days he was the lender to you. Then, he hands this check for $9,500 to a third party from whom he buys raw materials, and this party deposits it and does not draw on it for three or four days. He is then doing the lending and so on it goes. If the bank does the lending, it would have to do it on the basis of its original capital and it cannot do this. Its own capital is taken up with the management of the clerical work and the buildings and its work as a middleman. It has no capital of its own to lend. The only capital it lends is other people's capital.

August 26, 1930

It is usual to point out today that saving is probably not done to a large extent for the sake of the interest. It is done for other reasons, because of some accumulative instinct. People want to make provision for future emergencies; they want to provide for the taking care of their children; or they save, because they are building up a business and have pride in the growth of that business. Some also save merely because they do not have time to spend all they get. Corporate saving is not closely connected with individual decisions. There is sometimes saving through governmental action, where the government taxes the people and devotes the proceeds to public works and durable goods. The interest is not the chief incentive to saving on the part of the poor and for the rich, the saving is very nearly automatic. With the middle classes, it is more nearly true that the reward for saving is in the form of interest, which acts as a real inducement. These people have ambitions and objectives that require certain sums, and if the rate of interest is changed, it changes the relative amount of annual income which they need to set aside. As has been pointed out, the savings curve is more likely to have a positive than a negative inclination.

Percent of income saved

If people have a fairly definite goal requiring a certain amount, such as providing for their children, the higher the interest rate, the smaller the amount of investment they need to make in order that it shall grow into that amount in a given period of time. In this case, the increase in interest rate will decrease rather than increase, the amount of saving. This breaks the ordinary connection supposed to exist between the interest rate and saving.

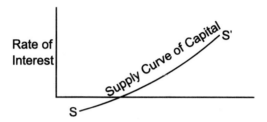

In the above diagram, *S-S'* represents the supply curve of capital. There is one factor, however, that does not tend to support this whole idea. There is an indirect connection between the rate of interest and the volume of saving. The great bulk of saving is made out of income from property; American income tax statistics and those of other countries show the percentage of income from property to the income from personal property rising sharply as the bulk of the saving rises. The bulk of saving is done by the rich, and the bulk of their income is property income. What that income shall be depends very much on the interest rate. The bigger their income, the more they save. If their income should double, their savings might quadruple or more. If we had personal information about the way in which the rich manage their finances, we could get some more systematic verifiable evidence, but so far, we have almost nothing of this sort available. We know much more about the budgetary habits of the poor than about those of the middle class and of the rich.

One field for investigation that promises to tell us something about the habits of the very rich is in court cases connected with inheritance taxation. In the court records of such cases, there is an attempt to show that some rich person disposed of a large part of his property in anticipation of death and not long before death, in order to evade estate taxes. Usually in such cases, it is necessary to present a little information regarding the financial habits of the deceased. In such cases, there is a body of information that could be worked up with interesting results.

Rent

There is one peculiarity in conventional rent theory as compared to the other factors in distribution. You start out at once in discussing rent with the realistic assumption that the factor is not a standardized one, that all the units may be taken as different, and that the differences rather than the similarities will be stressed. Instead of speaking of units of land, one speaks of the differences in fertility or a situation of different pieces of land. This difference in emphasis explains a good deal of the difference in the theorizing. The theorizing with regard to land is not nearly as different as it looks. It does, however, look quite different from that of a standard wage per unit of labor or an interest rate per unit of liquid and homogeneous capital.

However, there is some empirical justification for this differentiation in approach. The differences in land are more permanent, and they are there from the start. Particular capital goods tend to become different from each other, but they start out precisely the same. In large-scale enterprises, labor of a given grade gets to be a pretty standardized commodity. An employer knows what he means by a thousand laborers. Particularly in the machine age, he can exact of them approximately the same output per unit of time and pay.

In the case of land, the differences are more striking and more important. The lack of standardization creates problems of its own kind. The chief controversy that has centered about rent theory is whether it is any different from the theory of return to capital, whether the differentiation between land and capital has any logical justification. The classification is warranted, not necessarily as a sole classification; classifications have no sense except in terms of what questions you are trying to answer. One cannot discuss classifications per se. It is impossible to appraise a classification except in terms of the questions to be answered.

The relationship of rent to price concerns economists the most. Ricardo has been interpreted as saying that rent does not enter into the cost of production, whereas the remuneration of the other factors does. I would challenge you to find that statement in Ricardo. He says that rent does not enter into *that* cost of production. It is this passage which has led many to hold that Ricardo had the marginal concept. The products of agriculture have their value determined by that cost which is the highest cost necessary in order to induce the given output. This is the marginal concept. It is the cost of an additional increment regardless of who produces it. The additional increment may not be produced by the marginal producers. Regardless of who produces the marginal unit, it is that unit whose cost is the marginal cost.

Ricardo denied that rent enters into the marginal cost and, since that was the price-determining cost, he denied that rent was a part of that cost which determines price. Economists who state that rent does not enter into cost mean the price-determining cost. Some of the classical economists were divided on this point. Malthus said that rent was a part of the cost and so did Adam Smith. Ricardo, James Mill, J. S. Mill, Marshall, and Taussig denied that rent affects price in the same way as the other factors affect price. The Austrian theory is the Ricardian rent theory generalized to all the factors.

It is sometimes objected, by Cassel for instance, that land has greater elasticity than the supply of capital or labor, because the capital and labor supply curves have negative elasticities, whereas the elasticity of the supply of land is zero. The only thing that is important is the logic by which the conclusions are reached. The conclusions that we reach are not important. It is a question of tools rather than of the products of the tools. Whatever the facts may be, they lead to a different supply situation for the different factors; if the supply of land were fixed and that of capital and labor were positively inclined, the Ricardian rent theory is sound and it is impossible to object to it. If the supply of land is fixed and the supply of capital and labor have negative inclinations, the Ricardian rent theory would still be true; it would still be true that rent would not be a price-determining cost, but the quantitative propositions emerging from it would be different.

However, let us assume for the moment that Ricardo was right and that the supply curves of labor and capital have positive inclinations. Let us suppose a product, say, corn is produced on land that can also produce wheat. The land is worth something for wheat and something for corn, depending on the piece of land. There may be some land that can command a higher rental as wheat land than as corn land. Let the price of wheat rise, other things remaining the same, and the rental value of land capable of growing wheat will rise for that purpose. Land will become more valuable for wheat growing than before. The land value for corn growing will remain the same. Therefore, there will be some land that will acquire a higher value for wheat growing than for corn growing. There will be a reduction in the output of corn because of the withdrawal of some land from corn cultivation. The increase in the rental cost and value for wheat purposes will raise the price of corn. This may be identified as the opportunity cost doctrine. J. S. Mill admitted this concession to rent as a price-determining cost.

In the Austrian law of costs, the supply of labor is fixed, but the supply of labor for making iron is not fixed; that is variable. It is necessary to pay labor at a certain rate to get it away from some other industry. It depends on what the industry can afford to pay and how many units it can hire.

If the land is available for different purposes, then even on the Ricardian assumption of a fixed supply of land in general, the rent that a piece of land can pay for one use will enter into the determination of the cost of production for the other use. The rent that land can get for purposes of growing wheat will help to determine the price of corn. The rent that land can get for growing corn will affect the price of wheat by affecting the supply of wheat.

Ricardo was usually a very poor expositor. He was elliptical, and very concise and brief. He sometimes did not state his assumptions at all. He took it for granted that all reasonable men would have them in mind. A large number of the so-called "corrections" that have since been made in Ricardo were made by contemporaries of Ricardo and were a part of the classical rent theory.

For land which is just on the margin, the price is clearly influenced by that rent. However, for land that is clearly superior in rent-producing power for one use rather than for the other, at least the excess is price determined and not price determining. If it were twice as much, it would not make any difference in the price of the product nor the extent of the production.

One writer who has not received all the attention he deserves because he was a journalist and people took it for granted that he wrote for the general public is Thompson, who was once editor of the *Westminster Review.*[39] The following are some of the propositions denied by Thompson in around the year 1830:

1. Rent appears because lands differ in quality.
2. Rent appears because additional units are produced at a higher cost.
3. The value of corn is regulated by the cost of producing that portion of the output which yields no rent. The marginal unit is a no-rent unit and the marginal unit is the price-determining one.

The following are Thompson's replies:

Rent is paid because corn is scarce relative to the demand. Corn is scarce because good land is scarce and, since there are diminishing returns to operations on good land, the existence of inferior land reduces rent rather than creates it. He uses the analogy of a reservoir with a leak in it. The reservoir is the rent of good land. The leak is the output of the poor land. The existence of the leak reduces the level of rent. In other words, the closer the poor land is in quality to the good land, the greater the output on the good land and the less the rent that the good land can command.

His statement that rent is not a component part of the price of a commodity is all right if it is meant that the rent is not the cause of the price of the produce, because the price of the produce is not the cause of the rent. That is what Ricardo meant. There can be rent even though there are no differences in the cost of different pieces of land. On the practical question of what the supply curve of land is like, I constantly run across instances in which men in contact with land are reasoning as if the supply curve of land does look different from that of the other factors. When they do not think of it in this way, they do not do so largely because they are not thinking of this ability to shift land from one use to another.

A question of fact on which I have no information but on which information would be significant is to what extent for different pieces of land there is a general technological option as to the sort of crops you can produce from them. What is the range of options for the same land that a typical American farmer has? If there were an option, in order to present the Ricardian rent theory in relation to price, it would be necessary that for the group of commodities as a whole, price is not determined by rent. For relative prices within the group, rent is a factor.

In truck gardening, the range of possible products is greater than in grain cultivation. On a typical farm in Iowa, what option has a farmer with land ordinarily used for growing corn? Wheat, oats, and soy beans are alternative crops, or the land can be used for pasture. Suppose there are six alternative crops; in order to maintain the Ricardian theory intact, you would still have to insist that the supply of land is fixed. The degree of variability in the supply of land is negligible. The land that is used is not of use for any other purpose except for these six crops. Land gets its uses solely from its marginal value for this group of uses. For this group of uses, the group price is not determined by rent, but the relative prices within the group are determined by the relative rent of the land. This is very much like the non-competing group concept with regard to wages. Within the group rent determines; as between the groups rent does not determine.

The Ricardian issue is really not so important with respect to relative prices of commodities. The concession which J. S. Mill himself made is that the rent which land can pay in growing wheat is a factor in determining the cost of corn.

An example of specialized land is most of the land in Wyoming and Nevada. Even here, there is a possibility of grazing cattle or grazing sheep. The relative prices of sheep and cattle would be affected by the relative rents that land would have for the other uses.

In distribution theory, the Ricardian propositions are more vital. It is a question of the supplies of the factors in production. Generally stated, the classical theory assumes that land will get a greater percentage of the total product. Longfield pointed out that this was not so.[40] All that we can say on a priori grounds is that the diminishing productivity curve is negatively inclined for the factors which are being increased; then, the constant factor will get an increased return, but one must not say that it will be increased sufficiently to give it a larger share in the new situation. All that can be said is that land will get more; it cannot be said how much more or whether it will get relatively more.

This is sometimes called the "historical law of diminishing returns." All that changes is an increase in the amount of labor and capital, with land remaining the same.

Ricardo's version placed more pessimistic emphasis on the matter than was called for. He said that land would get a greater share rather than a greater absolute amount. In the nineteenth century, technological discovery was such as to create a new economic rent. It has reduced the importance of differentials in the quality and situation of land. The invention of the steel locomotive, which has brought the western area of the United States into the market, has meant a significant contribution to the European supply of grain. Technological improvement has tended more to decrease the importance of rent than to increase it. There is some likelihood that actual research would show that the actual historical process has been the reverse of what has been predicted by the classical economists. Not much blame can be placed on them, however, for not seeing that the Industrial Revolution would lower transportation costs more than other things. This factor made the Mississippi Valley a significant factor in providing the European countries with food. This resulted in cutting down rents throughout the entire world.

What results you reach with respect to the relationship between rent and price depends on the assumptions with which you start out. One should guard against stating one's conclusions without any assumptions, as if there were an answer to the problem without assumptions. Is the Ricardian theory being spoken of, or if the actual facts are being spoken of, what are the facts?

The important phase of the problem is for distribution theory, and there a great deal depends on the relative elasticity of the supplies of the factors or production. It is important to know what the supply curves of capital and labor are like.

An English gentleman's farm is likely to be his estate, his hunting grounds, his recreation park, and the source of his income. A lot of the land has a potential value as residential property so that it does not get its value from its current yield. Even so, rents seem to be lower in England now than in 1840 in spite of the depreciated monetary unit. The technological factors have worked to more than offset a greater increase in the physical amount of capital and labor in England than in the amount of land available for use in England.

August 27, 1930

Marshall avoids circular reasoning by a simultaneous distribution theory. The method of showing how equilibrium will be reached is extremely difficult. The Mathematical School on the whole has not seriously attempted to cope with this problem. Chapter 5 of Cassel is a simplification of the Mathematical School's approach; he does not, however, state how equilibrium is reached, but just tells us that when equilibrium is reached, things will be the way he describes them to be.

One way of pointing out how equilibrium can be reached when you are not quite at it is by the method of partial differentiation. This is essentially the neoclassical method of assuming that other things remain the same except for one factor which is changed. The statistician would say that the neoclassical school does this by brute force and such that they cannot operate on actual problems on that basis.

There is no circular reasoning of the vicious sort in the Lausanne School of approach. The Marshallian approach is fundamentally the same as this school of approach except when Marshall is dealing with such a question as the effect of a small increase of labor on the general distribution. The effect is the same except that in the Lausanne School, it is necessary to state in terms of equations just what things are being kept constant and at what levels they are being kept constant; for Marshall, his demand schedule indicates the schedule of quantities which would be taken at a given schedule of prices, which are what they happen to be. This is implicit in Marshall. This proposition is in the Mathematical School explicitly. I understand that this is the method used in Taylor's theorem in calculus, which was introduced into economics by Cournot.[41] This is the ability to differentiate one term when all the others are kept unaltered.

Marshall may speak of changes in rent without reference to changes in wages, but that is again to be regarded as referring only to small changes in rent and, therefore, to this method of assuming other things constant, which is the partial differentiation principle.

There is a vicious circle in all economic analysis where it comes into conflict with the doctrine that all things are mutually dependent. The hope is always that the degree of error introduced is negligible.

Profits

I rarely get to profits theory. Most of what has been done with profits theory is negligible. Only two economists have dealt with it in a penetrating manner. One of these is Schumpeter, and the other is Knight.[42]

Seager used to distinguish between two types of profits theories: risk theories and change theories, those explaining reward for assumption of risk and those explaining profits as due to presumably unpredictable change.[43] However, these are the same thing. Without change, there would be no risk and it is change which produces the risk.

Knight distinguishes between predictable and unpredictable changes. If you exclude out of profits interest and the wages of management, the reward to the individual entrepreneur is the pure profit, excluding also what is paid to an insurance company for the assumption of risk. What is left is what the Germans speak of as *konjunctur* incomes. Whatever comes from this situation is profits. They may be negative or positive. In this sense, profits is a residual share.

In the purely static state, some have maintained that there would be no profits and that there would be no unpredictable changes. Entrepreneurs would get the current rate of interest on their investment, the wages of management, and that is all. Would there not be fires in the static state, and would it not be possible that some would have insured against them and others would not, and, therefore, would there be losses on the part of those who had not? Would not others who had not insured make a profit on the premiums, because they would not have any fires? You can assume a static state in which there is constant equilibrium or statistical equilibrium. For instance, all the fish in a balanced aquarium may not be of the same age and size, but there is a maintenance of the same average of all the factors in the situation.

In a case of this sort, it is possible to have bankruptcies and receiverships in the static state, but they will be static in the statistical sense. For instance, the total crop for all farmers will be the same each year.

There will be individual variations within the group but for the group as a whole, the output shall be constant. Under these circumstances, there could be profits in the static state. There might be profits for Jones, but there would be equivalent negative profits for Smith and there would be no profits as a whole.

In a statistically static state, each individual faces a certain amount of business risk. He does not know what will happen to himself. The degree of risk being known, he could pay an actuarial premium and protect himself against that risk, but suppose he does not insure. Does it follow that he will go into that industry in which there is that degree of risk if he knows that on the average, he may expect a return which during a course of years on the average would just offset these possible losses? Would he take a chance of extra gain each year equivalent to the chance of loss? That is a question of fact. Jones might win but Smith would have to lose to the same amount.

Any lottery, horse race, or Monte Carlo has to be based on the principle of charging the individual at a higher price than the actual value of his chance. On the same basis, it has been said that gold mining has not paid the going returns. This would be more true for small-scale mining.

The chance of a big gain will be more overvalued than the chance of a moderate gain. In the case of a lottery, it is advisable to have two or three big prizes rather than a lot of small prizes. In the English and Australian sweepstakes, there are relatively few prizes and these are huge ones. These sweepstakes give less for the money than do the Latin-American or bootlegged American ones that have a great many prizes, but smaller ones.

Are business men governed by this same sort of psychology? This is a thing to which we do not know the answer, and it would be an extremely difficult thing to find out or to think out a way of finding out whether on the whole, risk taking is a net deterrent to the business world.

For most insurance companies, the load factor must run probably close to 50 percent. Thus, the load factor costs twice as much as the actuarial risk to insure against it. That is a proof that business men regard certain types of risks as risks that should be avoided even at more than their worth on an actuarial basis. This is because there is the absence of the big prize phase. What one gains if he does not have a fire is just the cost of the premiums, and this is not spectacular. For many types of gains and losses, the business man will assume a risk even though the prospects of reward are not as great as the prospects of loss.

Not many industries hedge; many business men hedge on foreign exchange, but that is because it seems so very mysterious both to business men and to students. Some risks business men assume as a matter of course, and others they welcome because they are accompanied by a chance of special profits, and others they scrupulously guard against.

It is poor business ethics to assume the fire risk. The fire risk is likely to be one that involves more than one's own profits. If a fire occurs, you are more than wiped out completely; your creditors may be wiped out too. It is a matter of moral code. A good many types of contracts will not be made unless there is a pledge or evidence that the man is insured against fire. In many contracts, one of the contracting parties gets the policy. In the case of a bank lending money on commodities, it always wants a fire insurance policy covering the goods. In the case of money lent on a house or a building, the lender will insist that he hold the insurance policy or that it be held by a third party. The historical explanation of this is that such a smashing loss is likely to hit one's creditors and not be absorbed in a personal loss to oneself. The code has been built up in this way in order to protect innocent third parties.

Underestimation is also an important element in explaining losses and an important element in making profits. The rain falls alike on the just and the unjust. In the same way, men may make greater profits than they anticipated when they entered into business. Ignorance may occasionally be bliss in business as well as in other activities.

Some economists have been trying to find out a way in which they could find whether risk taking is in the nature of a deterrent or an attraction to business men.

In different regions and different countries, men have different degrees of venturesomeness. In the United States, men will ordinarily take business risks at a higher ratio of their actuarial value than north of England business men or Scotch business men, and on the continent, they will be still more conservative. Part of the American prosperity may be due to this greater venturesomeness. There is a question of whether on the whole the United States loses or gains by this venturesomeness. There is great waste; it is seen in the obsolescence of machinery after five or ten years of use and in the great number of bankruptcies. However, we gain in the way in which we adapt new methods to American conditions. On net, do we gain or lose?

The theory of profits corresponding to the Ricardian theory of rent has a differential for superior skill in risk taking, a wages of management. The real profits, the pure profits, is not the reward for skillful risk taking, but is simply the return for risk taking where you have taken a gambling chance, such as in the case of a roulette wheel. Pure profits is the net income of what one gets when he is lucky over what he has paid for the chance of playing. Skill gets a reward like a wage. What pure chance brings one is the pure profits notion to be distinguished from the wages of superintendence or the wages or risk or of management.

Profits are the wages of risk taking, but not of risk judging. If a man is willing to pay $10 for one chance in two of winning $18, there are no net profits, but there are net business losses. The risk takers, as a whole, lose. It is not a two-sided proposition. You are gambling with circumstances, and it is not necessary that anybody shall gain. The ordinary statistical data that you would get would enable you to throw out extreme hypotheses, but they would not enable you to come to a definite conclusion. Book records as to profits are weird things. In order to understand them, it is necessary to know the history of that set of books. The profits may be either an exaggeration or a gross estimate. It is also necessary to apply current rates of return in order to know whether there are any excesses or deficits. We are not ready, therefore, on the basis of known conclusions, to come to any definite conclusions about these questions.

In the terms of a dynamic state, meaning a state that is undergoing constant change in an unpredictable way, profits are an unpredictable element in a world in which change occurs in an unpredictable way. Profits are basically a sort of remainder item in the sense that all errors and mismanagement and unanticipated events exhaust their influence on the profits item before they can be extended to any other items. The profit taker is the residual risk taker. He bears the first impact of loss and is the last to be assured of his income. Whatever chance occurs, favorable or unfavorable, affects him, while it may not affect any other participant in the enterprise.

So ends the lesson.

Notes

1. Ed.: Nassau William Senior (1831) and John Ramsay McCulloch (1825).
2. Ed.: W.T. Thornton (1869) and J.S. Mill (1869).
3. Ed.: Harriet Martineau (1832).
4. Ed.: F.A. Walker (1883).
5. Ed.: Rev. John McVickar (1825), Candy Raguet (1839).
6. Ed.: Henry Vethake (1838), Simon Newcomb (1886), John Rae (1834).
7. Ed.: Arthur Twining Hadley (1897).
8. Ed.: J.B. Clark (1899).
9. Ed.: J.E. Cairnes (1857).
10. Ed.: Johann Heinrich von Thünen (1826) and Mountifort Longfield (1834).

11. Ed.: John A. Hobson (1900).
12. Ed.: Thorstein Veblen (1908).
13. Ed.: Sydney J. Chapman (1911).
14. Ed.: Irving Fisher (1930).
15. Ed.: Ferdinand Lasalle, as attributed by Karl Marx in his *Critique of the Gotha Programme* 1875).
16. Ed.: John Stuart Mill (1871 [1909]).
17. Ed.: J. E. Cairnes (1874).
18. Ed.: This is likely a reference to the Economics 303 class, "Current Tendencies," which was taught by both Viner and Frank Knight (including one time, together) during this period.
19. Ed.: Gustav Cassel (1923).
20. Ed.: Vilfredo Pareto (1897).
21. Ed.: Francis YsidroEdgeworth (1881).
22. Ed.: Francis Galton (1869).
23. Ed.: Ethel Elderton and Karl Pearson (1910).
24. Ed.: Lewis Terman (1916).
25. Ed.: William Thomas Thornton (1869).
26. Ed.: Friedrich von Wieser (1925).
27. Ed.: Irving Fisher (1930).
28. Ed.: John Bates Clark (1899).
29. Ed.: John Bates Clark (1899), chap.IX, para. 28.
30. Ed.: Böhm-Bawerk (1891).
31. Ed.: EugenBöhm-Bawerk (1890).
32. Ed.: Thomas Manley (1669).
33. Ed.: Charles W. Mixter (1899).
34. Ed.: Thomas N. Carver (1904).
35. Ed.: Adolphe Landry (1904).
36. Ed.: Henry L. Moore (1914).
37. Ed.: Edwin Cannan (1928).
38. Ed.: A. B. Wolf (1920).
39. Ed.: Thomas Perronet Thompson (1826).
40. Ed.: Mountifort Longfield (1834).
41. Ed.: A. A. Cournot (1838).
42. Ed.: Joseph A. Schumpeter (1912) and Frank H. Knight (1921).
43. Ed.: Henry R. Seager (1913).

Appendix[*]:
Assignments in Viner's Economics 301

(In Order of Assignment)

Marshall, Bk III, chap. 3, 4

Bohm-Bawerk, Positive Theory of Capital, Bk IV, chap. 4

Schultz, Meaning of Statistical Demand Curves, 1–10, 25–41

Marshall, Bk V, chap. 3, 4, 5, 12, App. H

Viner, Cost Curves

Cunynghame, Geometrical Political Economy, chap. 3

Smart, Introduction to the Theory of Val., 64–83

B. B., Ultim Stand. Of Val., Ann. of Am. Ac., Sept. 1894

    One word More on Ult. S. of V., Econ. Jour., Dec. 1894

Marshall, Bk. V, chap. 6

    Bk. V, chap. 14

Viner, Objective Tests of Comp. Pr. appl, to the Cem. Ind JPE, '25

J. S. Mill, Outline of Pol Ec., Bk II, chap. 11, sec. 1; Bk I, chap. 6, sec.[1]

Henry George, Progress and Poverty, Bk I, chap. 1, 3, 4.

F. W. Taussig, Principles, Vol II, chap. 39, 51.

J. B. Clark, Distr. of Wealth, chap. 1, 7, 8, preface.

F. A. Walker, Pol. Ec., Part IV, chap. 4, 5. Part VI, Sec. 5

Adam Smith, Bk. I, chap. 10

J. S. Mill, Bk II, chap. 14

Cairnes, Pol. Ec., Part I, chap. 3, arts. 4, 5

Taussig, chap. 47

J. B. Clark, chap. 9, 13

B. B., Bk. II, chap. 1–5; Bk. V, chap. 1–4; Bk. VI, chap. 1, 2, 4, 5, 6
     Bk. VII, chap. 1, 2

Marshall, Bk. VI, chap. 9

Ogilvie, Marshall on Rent, Econ. Journ., March 1930

J. B. Clark, chap. 23

Notes

*   Viner's reading list is reproduced exactly from the document that the editors have in their possession. Bibliographic information related to these readings is contained in the reference list that follows this appendix.

1.   Mill's text, of course, is titled *Principles of Political Economy*. The section number for the reading from of Book I, chapter 6 referred to here is not shown on the document that the editors possess.

References

Böhm-Bawerk, Eugen von. 1890. *Capital and Interest: A Critical History of Economical Theory.* Trans. with a preface by William Smart. New York: Macmillan.

———. 1891. *Positive Theory of Capital.* Trans. with a preface and analysis by William Smart. New York: G.E. Stechert.

———. 1894. "One Word More on Ultimate Standard of Value." *Economic Journal* 4 (December): 719–24.

Böhm-Bawerk, Eugen von, and C. W. Macfarlane. 1894. "The Ultimate Standard of Value." *Annals of the American Academy of Political and Social Science* 5 (September): 1–60.

Cairnes, J. E. 1857. *The Character and Logical Method of Political Economy.* London: Longman.

———. 1874. *Some Leading Principles of Political Economy Newly Expounded.* London: Macmillan.

Cannan, Edwin. 1928. *Wealth: A Brief Explanation into the Causes of Economic Wealth.* 3rd ed. London: P.S. King.

Carver, Thomas N. 1904. *The Distribution of Wealth.* New York: Macmillan.

Cassel, Gustav. 1923. *The Theory of Social Economy.* New York: Harcourt Brace.

Chapman, Sydney J. 1911. *Outlines of Political Economy.* London: Longmans.

Clark, John Bates. 1899. *The Distribution of Wealth.* New York: Macmillan.

Cournot, Antoine Augustine. 1838. *Recherches sur les principes mathématiques de la théorie des richesses.* Paris: Chez L. Hachette.

Cunynghame, H. 1904. *Geometrical Political Economy.* Oxford: Clarendon Press.

Davenport, Herbert Joseph. 1910. *Value and Distribution: A Critical and Constructive Study.* Chicago, IL: University of Chicago Press.

Edgeworth, Francis Ysidro. 1881. *Mathematical Psychics.* London: C. Kegan Paul.

———. 1911. "Contributions to the Theory of Railway Rates—II." *Economic Journal* 21 (December): 551–71.

Elderton, Ethel M., and Karl Pearson. 1910. *A First Study of the Influence of Parental Alcoholism on the Physique and Ability of the Offspring.* 2nd ed. London: Dulau.

Fawcett, Henry. 1863. *Manual of Political Economy.* London: Macmillan.

Fetter, Frank A. 1915. *Economic Principles.* New York: The Century.

Fisher, Irving. 1892. *Mathematical Investigations in the Theory of Value and Prices. Transactions of the Connecticut Academy* IX (July). Repr. Yale University Press, 1895.

———. 1930. *The Theory of Interest.* New York: Macmillan.

Galton, Francis. 1869. *Hereditary Genius.* London: Macmillan.

George, Henry. 1879 *Progress and Poverty.* New York: D. Appleton.

Hadley, Arthur Twining. 1897. *Economics: An Account of the Relations between Private Property and Public Welfare.* New York: G. Putnam's Sons.

Hobson, John A. 1900. *The Economics of Distribution.* London: Macmillan.

Jevons, William Stanley. 1871. *The Theory of Political Economy.* London: Macmillan.

Knight, Frank H. 1921. *Risk, Uncertainty, and Profit.* New York: Houghton Mifflin.

Landry, Adolphe. 1904. *L'Intérèt du Capital.* Paris: V. Gerard & E. Brière.

Lloyd, W. F. 1834. *A Lecture on the Notion of Value.* London: Roake and Varty.

Laughlin, James Laurence. 1887. *Elements of Political Economy.* New York: D. Appleton.

Longfield, Mountifort. 1834. *Lectures on Political Economy.* Dublin: Richard Milliken and Son.

MacVane, S. M. 1890. *The Working Principles of Political Economy in a New and Practical Form: A Book for Beginners.* New York: Effingham Maynard.

Manley, Thomas. 1669. *Usury at Six Percent Examined.* London: T. Radcliffe.

Marshall, Alfred. 1920. *Principles of Economics.* 8th ed. London: Macmillan.

Martineau, Harriet. 1832. *Illustrations of Political Economy.* 9 vols. London: Charles Fox.

McCulloch, J. R. 1823. "Wages." *Encyclopedia Britannica.*

———. 1825. *Principles of Political Economy.* London: John Murray.

McVickar, John. 1825. *Outlines of Political Economy.* New York: Wilder & Campbell.

Mill, J. S. 1869a. "Thornton on Labour and Its Claims, Part I." *Fortnightly Review* 29 (May): 505–18.

———. 1869b. "Thornton on Labour and Its Claims, Part II." *Fortnightly Review* 30 (June): 680–700.

———. 1871/1909. *Principles of Political Economy.* Ed. with an introduction by W. J. Ashley, 7th ed. London: Longmans, Green, 1909.

Mixter, C. W. 1899. "The Theory of Savers' Rent and Some of Its Applications." *Quarterly Journal of Economics* 13 (April): 245–69.

Moore, Henry L. 1914. *Economic Cycles: Their Law and Cause.* New York: Macmillan.

Newcomb, Simon. 1886. *Principles of Political Economy.* New York: Harper & Brothers.

Nicholson, J. Shield. 1893. *Principles of Political Economy.* London: Adam and Charles Black.

Ogilvie, F. W. 1930. "Marshall on Rent." *Economic Journal* 40 (March): 1–24.

Pigou, A. C. 1920. *The Economics of Welfare.* London: Macmillan.

Rae, John. 1834. *Statement of Some New Principles on the Subject of Political Economy.* Boston, MA: Hilliard, Gray.

Raguet, Candy. 1839. *A Treatise on Currency and Banking.* London: Ridgway.

Schultz, Henry. 1930. *The Meaning of Statistical Demand Curves.* University of Chicago (Privately Printed).

Schumpeter, Joseph A. 1921. *Theorie der wirtschaftlichen Entwicklung.* Munich and Leipzig: Duncker and Humblot. English translation: *The Theory of Economic Development. An Inquiry into Profits, Capital, Credit, Interest, and the Business Cycle.* Cambridge: Harvard University Press, 1934.

Seager, Henry R. 1913. *Principles of Economics.* New York: Henry Holt.

Secrist, Horace. 1924. *Expense Levels in Retailing: A Study of the "Representative Firm" and of "Bulk-Line Costs in the Distribution of Clothing.* Chicago, IL: Northwestern University School of Commerce, Bureau of Business Research, Series 2, No. 9.

Senior, Nassau. 1831. *Three Lectures on the Rate of Wages.* London: John Murray.

Schultz, Henry. 1928. *Statistical Laws of Demand and Supply with Special Application to Sugar.* Chicago: University of Chicago Press.

Smart, William. 1910. *Introduction to the Theory of Value.* 2nd ed. London: Macmillan.

Smith, Adam. 1776. *An Inquiry into the Nature and Causes of the Wealth of Nations.* Oxford: Oxford University Press, 1976.

Taussig, Frank W. 1911. *Principles of Economics.* New York: Macmillan. 2nd ed., 1915.

———. 1919. "Price-Fixing as Seen by a Price-Fixer." *Quarterly Journal of Economics* 33 (February): 205–41.

Thompson, Thomas Perronet. 1826. *An Exposition of the Fallacies of Rent, Tithes, &c. Containing an Examination of Mr. Ricardo's Theory of Rent. Being in the Form of a Review of the Third Edition of Mr. Mill's Elements of Political Economy.* London: Hatchard and Son.

Thorton, William Thomas. 1869. *On Labour, Its Wrongful Claims and Rightful Dues, Its Actual Present and Possible Future.* London: Macmillan.

Thünen, Johann Heinrich von. 1826. *Der Isolierte Staat in Beziehung auf Landwirtschaft und Nationaloekonomie.* English ed.: *The Isolated State.* Trans. Carla M. Wartenberg, ed. with an introduction by Peter Hall. New York: Pergamon Press.

Veblen, Thorstein. 1908. "Professor Clark's Economics." *Quarterly Journal of Economics* 22 (February): 147–95.

Vethake, Henry. 1838. *The Principles of Political Economy.* Philadelphia, PA: P. H. Nicklin & T. Johnson.

Viner, Jacob. 1925. "Objective Tests of Competitive Price Applied to the Cement Industry." *Journal of Political Economy* 33 (February): 107–11.

———. 1932. "Cost Curves and Supply Curves." *Zeitschrift für Nationalökonomie* 3 (September): 23–46.

Walker, F. A. 1883. *Political Economy.* American Science Series: Advanced Course. New York: Henry Holt. 3rd ed., revised and enlarged, 1892.

Walras, Léon. 1874. *Éléments d'économie politique pure, ou théorie de la richesse sociale.* Lausanne: L. Corbaz.

Wicksteed, Philip H. 1910. *The Common Sense of Political Economy.* London: Macmillan.

Wieser, Friedrich von. 1892. "The Theory of Value (A Reply to Professor MacVane)." *Annals of the American Academy of Political and Social Science* 2 (March): 24–52.

———. 1927. *Social Economics* [Translation of *Theorie der gesellschaftlichen wirtschaft* (1914)]. New York: Greenberg.

Wolf, A. B. 1920. "Savers' Surplus and the Interest Rate." *Quarterly Journal of Economics* 35 (November): 1–35.

Index

CPSIA information can be obtained at www.ICGtesting.com
Printed in the USA
LVOW121913300413

331703LV00006B/35/P

9 781412 851664